SLOW LIFE
BY SIX SENSES

KATE O'BRIEN / Text
JÖRG SUNDERMANN / Photography

SLOW LIFE BY SIX SENSES

SUSTAINABLE • LOCAL • ORGANIC • WHOLESOME • LEARNING • INSPIRING • FUN • EXPERIENCES

EDITIONS DIDIER MILLET

Chess set made from local sustainable wood in a pool villa at Six Senses Destination Spa-Phuket.
OPPOSITE: Relax in a hammock over the crystal-blue sea at Soneva Gili by Six Senses, Maldives.
TITLE PAGE (FROM LEFT): Locally-crafted fish-shaped hooks in the bathroom of a Six Senses resort; a dramatic sea view from Six Senses Hideaway Yao Noi, Thailand.
HALF-TITLE PAGE: Vibrant marine life abounds around Soneva Gili by Six Senses, Maldives.

Executive Editor
MELISA TEO

Editor
LAURA DOZIER

Designer
CHAN HUI YEE

Production Manager
SIN KAM CHEONG

Photography Director
MELISA TEO

Photographer's Assistant
LI YUEMIN

Project Director for Six Senses
RAYMOND HALL

Environment Conscience
ARNFINN OINES

Chef
REMON ALPHENAAR

SIX SENSES RESORTS & SPAS
19/F Two Pacific Place
142 Sukhumvit Road
Bangkok 10110, Thailand
www.sixsenses.com

The acronym SLOW LIFE is a Service Mark (SM) of Six Senses Resorts & Spas.

First published in 2009 by
EDITIONS DIDIER MILLET PTE LTD
121 Telok Ayer Street
#03-01, Singapore 068590
www.edmbooks.com

Photography © Six Senses Resorts & Spa
© 2009 Editions Didier Millet Pte Ltd

Printed in Singapore by Tien Wah Press

ISBN: 978-981-4217-38-5

CONTENTS

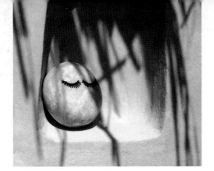

SLOW LIFE
There is more to life than increasing its speed.
- Mohandas Mahatma Gandhi

We are living in unusual times. We have dizzying amounts of information at our fingertips. We travel the globe with ease and can view any point on its surface through our computer screens. Surely there cannot be many surprises left? But there are, as humanity confronts its greatest challenge—the rising tide of climate change. Humans have exploited the earth without counting the cost, and unless we do something fast, how can its beauty survive intact to be enjoyed by future generations? People are increasingly voicing concern about the environment, climate change, sustainable practices, the quality of our food and much more; they are seeking a change but remain uncertain as to how they can address these issues and make a real difference in their lifetimes.

We are politically, economically and morally obliged to create a new world order, and SLOW LIFE explains how. SLOW LIFE is an acronym that represents the following ideals:

- Sustainable • Local • Organic • Wholesome
- Learning • Inspiring • Fun • Experiences

More than just words, these elements of SLOW LIFE are a prescription for being at the forefront of responsible living and environmental sustainability. The principles of SLOW LIFE offer the support, knowledge and guidance that we need to help us rediscover a cleaner, better and healthier world.

By appreciating where the key challenges lie, we can offer meaningful solutions. The food we choose, the clothes we wear, the cars we drive and the places we visit—when combined, all of these minute but important decisions that we make in the home and the workplace can bring about real change—one person, one step at a time. SLOW LIFE is not about doing everything at a snail's pace; rather, it is about actively reducing the ecological footprints of our lives and being fair custodians of our earth. It encourages us to live life rather than rush through it. SLOW LIFE is a very modern concept that learns from the past while embracing the future, and it is spreading fast.

SUSTAINABLE A sustainable society is one that does not destroy the foundations upon which it is built. It satisfies the needs of the present without compromising the ability of future generations to meet their needs. Sustainability is about finding solutions to problems without creating new problems.

FROM TOP: The "do not disturb" sign at Six Senses Destination Spa-Phuket is made of local stone on which closed eyelids are playfully inscribed; the stunning cliff-top restaurant at Six Senses Hideaway Zighy Bay, Oman. OPPOSITE: Wooden bridge leading to the observatory at Soneva Fushi by Six Senses, Maldives. PREVIOUS: Guests can enjoy the marine life right outside their villa at Soneva Gili by Six Senses, Maldives.

Sustainable produce, for instance, has no long-lasting negative impact on the earth and can be easily replenished. The successful businesses of the future will be those with bold and sustainable visions, entering uncharted territory and showing that such visions pay financially, socially and ecologically. The real beauty of sustainability is that it can be adapted to everything from economic development to food production, minimising the ecological footprints of our all-consuming lifestyles.

LOCAL From food to culture, clothing, employment and much more, striving to maximise the use of local resources is key to a sustainable future. For instance, the creation and consumption of fresh seasonal food—local food—cooked in accordance with each person's culture and produced and distributed in a way that does not jeopardise the earth's and mankind's balance is an ideal scenario, where local ways and resources are cherished. Focusing on local, rather than imported goods and services, not only significantly reduces our ecological footprints but also increases pleasure, as we celebrate what makes each part of the world unique while also enjoying food at its best and tastiest.

ORGANIC With respect to agriculture, organic is defined as an ecological production management system that promotes and enhances biodiversity, biological cycles and soil activity. Organic systems recognise that our health is directly connected to the food we eat and, ultimately, the health of the soil. According to the principles of SLOW LIFE, organic food production works in perfect tune with nature, and the quality of produce results from the quality of the environment: nature yields her most vibrant, balanced and flavoursome produce when farmed using pure organic practices. A wealth of research is showing that the organic concept is catching on as people seek cleaner, safer and more authentic food. Also, in terms of SLOW LIFE, the word organic refers to an improved way of living, one that rejects toxic chemicals and poor air quality and embraces organically derived fabrics, a healthier environment and a more holistic metaphor for life.

WHOLESOME From a food perspective, the most wholesome foods are those raised free from chemical processing and eaten at their most nutritious and delicious, as close as possible to where they were grown. However, the word wholesome implies far more. A wholesome life is spent enjoying fulfilling pleasures, being nurtured by sustainable, non-polluting practices, and a wholesome attitude is one that maintains a reverence for all living things. Looking to the wholesome offers a vibrant vision for a healthier, more centred and focused being.

LEARNING-INSPIRING-FUN-EXPERIENCES When adopting the SLOW LIFE, Mother Nature is the inspiration; the simplest of life's pleasures—be it a hike through nature's final frontiers or tasting the sweet ripeness of a freshly picked summer tomato—are all opportunities to learn and take stock of exactly what is at stake. Children are indeed our future, but in SLOW LIFE they are our present too. By performing leading roles in inspiring, fun experiences, children can be equipped with the tools to help them become intelligent guardians of the earth.

It is now accepted that the primary cause of our diminishing natural resources is human greed. We can have as much impact on the solution as we have had on the problems. It is said that everyone is the same when they dream. We all dream, many of us vividly. Help make this dream for a responsible, environmentally and socially sustainable future a reality in our lifetime. Slow living is here. Embrace it and keep it SLOW for LIFE.

FROM TOP: A selection of freshly prepared traditional southern Thai relishes with crunchy vegetables; a mountain-top picnic close to Six Senses Hideaway Zighy Bay, Oman.
OPPOSITE: The inspiring view from outside a water villa overlooking the infinity-edge pool and the sea at Six Senses Hideaway Ninh Van Bay, Vietnam.

A SUSTAINABLE PLANET: THE CALL FOR CHANGE

By educating ourselves and others, by doing our part to minimise our use and waste of resources, by becoming more active politically and demanding change, each one of us can make a difference. Perhaps more important, we each need to assess our own relationship to the natural world and renew a connection to it.

-Al Gore, Earth in the Balance: Ecology and the Human Spirit

Wilderness and wildness are precious commodities. As cities continue to expand, deeply inspiring natural sites are becoming increasingly rare. Tibet, for instance, is an area of jaw-dropping natural beauty, crossed by the greatest of Asian rivers—the Yangtze, the Mekong, the Brahmaputra and the Indus—but even amidst this raw wildness, the impact of human intervention is posing serious problems. Deforestation through industrial clear-cutting has already claimed much of Tibet's virgin forests. And the problems do not end there, of course. The environmental issues that we face in all areas of the world are poised to increase dramatically. It is predicted that as much as 80 percent of new energy demand in the next decade will come from China, India and other developing nations, so putting the brakes on environmental destruction will prove even more difficult.

However, in response to these mounting issues, the green movement has evolved from isolated protests to a global assault on our entire economic and political system. It is no longer a hippy's call for saving the forests and whales; it has become an urgent message about being responsible for our future. While we know that human actions have caused vast destruction, many people are reconnecting with nature and striving to protect it. Science is attacking the problem more aggressively than ever, but more importantly, individuals are also beginning to tip the carbon scales.

We already know the fastest, least expensive way to slow climate change: use less energy. With little effort, most of us could improve our energy diets by 25 percent or more—mainly by wasting less energy at home and on the road. A movement that starts with an efficient light bulb can change the world. If we are concerned about social and environmental justice, we have a moral obligation to do something, to work towards a harmonious relationship with the earth. So, what is holding us back?

As human populations soar, overcrowded cities can wreak havoc on the local environment with their insatiable demand for resources and the accompanying pollution. OPPOSITE: In Tibet, the Yarlung Zangbo River, the highest major river in the world, cuts a winding path through a wild, untouched landscape. PREVIOUS: Melting ice floating on water in the Weddell Sea, Antarctica.

Increasingly severe droughts caused by global warming could have disastrous effects, similar to this apocalyptic-looking scene in Cowra, Australia.
OPPOSITE (FROM TOP): Rampant deforestation in Madagascar has caused trees like this baobab tree to become increasingly rare; the Galapagos giant tortoise struggled with intensive hunting and the introduction of predators by humans, but now, due to conservation efforts, the largest member of the tortoise family is thriving again.

CURRENT CHALLENGES In our
increasingly integrated world, the implications of our behaviour are reaching further than we might think, beyond devastating effects on the natural world to troubling issues in the political arena. The energy we consume and the goods we buy involve us inadvertently in many of the world's most pressing issues, from catastrophic events related to climate change to oppressive governments profiting from inhumane and illegal activities. The challenges we face are complex and varied, to the extent that the war against climate change is one that must be fought on many fronts.

INDUSTRIALISATION From the time of the
steam engine, people in the industrialised world learned to live beyond the raw material limits of their immediate surroundings and became extremely rich by doing so. The Industrial Revolution, which was powered by cheap, plentiful fossil fuels, started to separate people from their environment. Burning coal, gas and oil meant that people could travel more frequently and faster, making the world seem smaller. There seemed to be no limit to the resources that could be exploited and the waste that could be dumped into the atmosphere, land, oceans and rivers. For more

than 200 years, humanity disregarded the few environmental warriors who warned about the grave danger of losing our link with nature. But, as these sustainability champions predicted, our all-consuming culture has taken its toll, and climate change is the planet's cry for help. GLOBALISATION Globalisation is a term encompassing the increasing integration of countries' individual economies, the rise in world trade, the impact on ordinary people of multi-national companies and the effect of large sums of money moving across borders. In addition to the economic dimension, globalisation also includes social, cultural, linguistic, political and environmental integration across national boundaries. The main difference between the past and today is that our current problems are truly global.

New global environmental challenges are a further consequence of globalisation, with climate change being the most imminent and obvious. Concern has been voiced that as countries compete to attract industry and jobs, environmental standards are compromised. While global integration has boosted demand and increased the flow of goods and services, institutions have been slow to adapt to the consequences of this immense assimilation. In the case of forests, for example, high-value timber is harvested, often illegally, and sold to the highest bidder with no consideration for sustainability, the indigenous wildlife that thrives in the forest or the native custodians whose livelihoods depend on these trees. Other problems include the exploitation of fisheries, persistent pollution, the spread of disease and the destruction caused by invasive alien species brought in by increased cross-border travel and trade.

Globalisation can be commended too. Communication, production and distribution are almost instantaneous: if a vaccine against a virus is required, it can be produced on a massive scale and delivered where it is most urgently needed, faster and more efficiently than ever before. Science has gone global with its breakthroughs, and new applications are being swiftly copied and shared. Also, new opportunities for environmental stewardship are created as the rapid spread of information and communication technology enhances environmental awareness and advocacy.

For instance, the launch of Google Ocean uncovered the underwater world of our planet's deepest oceans to virtual voyagers and conservation experts. The International Union for Conservation of Nature (IUCN), a key collaborator on Google's initiative, created the marine-protected area layer of the program, which contains information on more than 4,500 protected sites spread around the globe. From the Great Barrier Reef to the Galapagos, anyone can dive in and explore their natural beauty, learn what threats these protected areas face and find out how they can help.

Scientists benefit from this technology as well. BirdLife International was part of the team of scientists that used Google Earth to uncover a remote patch of pristine forest, home to a new species of butterfly, snake and globally threatened birds. Additionally, NGOs and conservation experts can combine satellite imagery with on-the-ground information to illustrate complex conservation issues more quickly and persuasively to decision makers. This has to be good. The key challenge, however, is to use the tools of globalisation in ways that support sustainable development.

As human populations swell, the level of our encroachment on nature increases as well, so that our negative influence can be seen in even the most beautiful of landscapes.
OPPOSITE: The awe-inspiring beauty of the natural world is seen even during nature's most violent moments.

POPULATION For most of our history, the human species lived as hunters and gatherers, a way of life that limited our population. With the development of agriculture, however, communities evolved that could support more individuals, and the people crisis began. The more human beings there are on the planet, the bigger our collective impact; our impact is felt in many ways, from soil erosion, over-fishing and deforestation to water shortages, loss of species and habitats. Most particularly, it is felt in terms of the rising emissions of carbon dioxide and other greenhouse gases with which humans are polluting the atmosphere.

James Lovelock highlights the gravity of the population problem in *The Revenge Of Gaia*, saying, "The root of our problems with the environment comes from a lack of constraint on the growth of the population. There is no single right number of people that we can have as a goal: the number varies with our way of life on the planet and the state of its health." This logic suggests that we must quickly adapt our way of life, especially since the United Nations has predicted that the world population will reach seven billion by early 2012 (up from the previous 6.8 billion estimate) and will surpass nine billion people by 2050. Most of the additional inhabitants will be in developing countries, whose populations are projected to rise from 5.6 billion to 7.9 billion by 2050.

What further damage will each person's footprint contribute to a planet that is already compromised? New energy-efficient and clean technology can help reduce the brunt of our impact. But at the moment, it is not enough to keep up with the current increase in human numbers and economic growth. While no one can accurately predict the future, many experts believe that if current patterns continue unabated, a crisis of humanity arising primarily from severe water shortages, droughts, hunger and disease will follow.

GLOBAL WARMING According to the United States Environmental Protection Agency, global temperatures have increased about 0.74°C (1.3°F) over the past century. Moreover, the National Oceanic and Atmospheric Administration (NOAA) reports that seven of the eight hottest years on record have occurred since 2001.

There is a solid scientific consensus that this rise in temperature is largely the result of the burning of fossil fuels and the release of greenhouse gases (carbon dioxide, methane and nitrous oxides in particular). As sunlight reaches earth, it is converted into infrared energy and emitted back through the atmosphere into space. Greenhouse gases absorb some of this energy, reducing the amount that is lost into space and warming the atmosphere. While these gases have always been present and the world's climate has always been in a state of flux, with ice ages and heat waves, our current predicament is primarily man-made.

Although future weather patterns are impossible to forecast, the Intergovernmental Panel on Climate Change (IPCC) predicts in its assessment "Climate Change 2007" a scenario where global temperatures increase about 0.2°C (0.4°F) per decade for the next two decades. The consequences of this type of increase would be dire. As islands in the Pacific disappear beneath the waves and polar ice caps melt, we can expect stronger hurricanes, harsher droughts, fiercer heat waves, heavier rains, shattered coastlines, higher sea levels and the extinction of many species.

GROSS NATIONAL HAPPINESS

At first glance, there appears to be a lack of governments prepared to make truly effective moves towards protecting the environment. However, there are inspirational policies at work today that offer a new perspective and suggest that any nation, no matter how small, can make a positive impact on the planet's health.

Gross National Happiness (GNH), for instance, is a term that was coined in 1972 by the fourth king of Bhutan, HM Jigme Singye Wangchuck. From the outset of His Majesty's reign, the collective pursuit of happiness became the goal of the country's development. The concept signalled his commitment to building an economy that would serve Bhutan's culture and environment.

The concept of GNH is based on the premise that the true development of human society takes place when material and spiritual development occur side by side. Hence, the four pillars of GNH are the promotion of sustainable development, preservation and promotion of cultural values, conservation of the natural environment and the establishment of good governance.

Coinciding with the coronation of His Majesty Jigme Khesar Namgyel Wangchuck (or King Khesar), fifth king of Bhutan in 2008, the Royal Government of Bhutan adopted the GNH index to reflect GNH values, set benchmarks and track the policies and performance of the country.

While other markers for a nation's health measure consumption and the production of goods (e.g. gross national product), the GNH attempts to offer a holistic measure of success, one that celebrates eco-friendly development and that, above all, is concerned with the wellbeing of its citizens. This revolutionary approach—which explicitly links the health of the environment to the health and happiness of the population—seems particularly significant now as many nations struggle to improve their relationship with the earth and stop climate change.

In a future where global warming causes severe storms with greater frequency, events like Hurricane Frances seen here crashing through Palm Beach, Florida, may become a much more common sight.
OPPOSITE: Children ride bikes through floodwaters in Jakarta, Indonesia.

GLOBAL SOLUTIONS

"On a global level, the overall picture is now clear and stark. Climate change is the overriding reality for the foreseeable future, forcing us to reconsider every aspect of our lives. It is now the greatest threat not just to our environment, but also to our human rights, public health, security and economic stability.

The Stern Review calls climate change the greatest and most far-reaching market failure ever. It is of course also a massive political and media failure too. Few people would have voted for policies causing it—and parties allowing it to happen—if properly informed of the risks, known for 30 years.

If not reversed it will cause mass migration on unimaginable scales as climate refugees seek asylum in countries they see as responsible for their predicament. This will require serious personal lifestyle changes. But these efforts will not be sufficient, and despair and frustration would follow when emissions continue rising.

Al Gore has said that, if we want to stop climate chaos, we must make it a moral issue. Slavery was once politically accepted and highly profitable. But a small group of individuals, mandated only by their conscience, found it humanly and morally unacceptable and managed to get it abolished. The suffragettes and civil rights movements also succeeded by turning their cause into a moral challenge.

Today the freedom, security and rights of all future generations are threatened by our actions. We are told that all values are relative, but that is not so. We all instinctively feel the responsibility to hand over a better—or at least not a worse—world to our children.

We must begin another Industrial Revolution, transforming our production and consumption, based on the circular 'cradle-to-cradle' loop models developed by Professor Michael Braungart in Germany [for more information, see page 37]. This challenge also offers the greatest business opportunity ever and will soon pit the true entrepreneurs against the defenders of privilege.

We need a new understanding of hierarchies of risk and danger. The ecological balance sheet is most important, for, while you can negotiate with financial creditors, you cannot negotiate with melting glaciers. Even the consequences of economic bankruptcies are soon overcome, while those of an environmental bankruptcy may last forever.

Our main challenge is to develop an integrated response. For example, energy efficiency requires ecological tax reform to provide the incentives needed to fulfil its potential. Wealth creation can no longer be built on destroying our real wealth—a healthy planet—in return for computer printouts claiming to tell us that we are the richest generation ever.

We need to develop early warning systems to stop us reaching negative tipping-points beyond which collapse can no longer be prevented. We also need 'early solution systems', identifying, developing and spreading future-proof policies and practices worldwide.

What we need to do will be very difficult—but the alternative is impossible. We need to work for both global justice and security, for one is impossible without the other. We need new institutions, e.g. an International Renewable Energy Agency (IRENA), now promoted by the German government, a Global Carbon Fund, and we need the World Future Council to continue speaking up for the interests of future generations. Human progress has always been underpinned by organisations. Visions need timetables.

There are huge opportunities here, especially in poorer countries. But they demand economies based on encouraging maturity and cooperation, not immaturity and greed. Optimised service delivery (not product ownership) will become the criterion of moral consumerism in a new world of mutual accountability. This accountability has to include the huge daily natural capital destruction caused by not using renewable energies to the maximum extent possible.

The huge potential abundance of solar energy shows that we can transmit to future generations values, traditions and societies that support the long-term flourishing of life on earth. We can and must build an economic, legal and institutional framework for the rapid re-construction of our energy, transport, agriculture and production systems and our industrial base.

We face unprecedented challenges, but to quote the US anti-slavery pioneer Reverend William Ellery Channing: 'There are times in history when to dare is the highest wisdom!'"

- Jakob von Uexküll, Founder, World Future Council

When human beings first began to take care of a plant food source, instead of simply foraging and gathering, when a clan started tending to its first berry patch, when farming was born, so was the manipulation of nature. Farmers all manipulate nature, some more than others. And some practices are more destructive than others. I may believe I can fool Mother Nature, but it's more as if she lets me get away with a few things.

- David Mas Masumoto, *Epitaph for a Peach*

Factory smoke filtering up into the cold winter sky in Harbin, China.
OPPOSITE: A Six Senses wind turbine in Tamil Nadu, India is designed to contribute to the offsetting of carbon emissions of Six Senses resorts and spas.

CARBON Carbon is the fourth most abundant element in the universe by mass after hydrogen, helium and oxygen. It is present in all known life forms and is the second most abundant element by mass (after oxygen) in the human body.

Carbon is passed from the atmosphere to living things (as carbon dioxide) and then returned to the atmosphere in the same form through a process known as the carbon cycle. Green plants remove carbon dioxide from the atmosphere by photosynthesis. The carbon then becomes part of the plant's energy system. Living organisms that consume plants or that consume organisms that eat plants return carbon dioxide to the atmosphere by respiration. Therefore, carbon is a key ingredient for creating our forests; it is the molecule at the bottom of our food chain, and carbon dioxide (CO_2) is one of the most significant greenhouse gases.

Each year, about 27 billion tonnes of carbon dioxide are belched out into the atmosphere. Of this approximately 7 billion is absorbed by oceans; 7 billion is taken up by forests and up to 13 billion accumulates in the atmosphere. However, in recent years, the accumulation of carbon dioxide in the atmosphere has risen faster than expected, to 18 billion tonnes. Scientists attribute this to humans producing more carbon dioxide. According to the Clean Air-Cool Planet's 2006 report (www.cleanair-coolplanet.org), a tonne of carbon dioxide is emitted if you:
• Fly 3,218 km (2,000 miles) in an airplane.
• Drive 2,173 km (1,350 miles) in an SUV
• Drive 9,656 km (6,000 miles) in a hybrid gasoline-electric car.
• Run an average US household for 60 days.

Moreover, climate change has compounded the problem. As the earth's temperature rises, the oceans and forests are less able to mop up the carbon dioxide. What's more, the ability of the oceans to dissolve atmospheric carbon dioxide is reduced too, with the overall result being a rise in sea levels, increased water temperatures and a change in ocean current patterns. This change in the oceans in turn causes loss of habitats, storms, droughts and flooding.

CARBON OFFSETTING It goes without saying that the best way to keep your carbon balance in check is by not emitting carbon, but offsetting is a useful way of dealing with unavoidable emissions, while putting the consequences of various choices clearly into focus. The repercussions of driving to work, flying to Fiji or leaving your air conditioning on all day become tangible. Managing our carbon balance sheet is a little like paying off debt with the ultimate goal being to stay in the black. How you choose to get there depends on your personal compass. For example, to offset 1,000 tonnes of carbon, you could:
• Run one 600-kilowatt wind turbine for a year.
• Replace 500 100-watt light bulbs with 18-watt compact fluorescent bulbs (10-year life).
• Replace 2,000 refrigerators with the highest efficiency model (10-year life).
• Protect 2 hectares (4 acres) of tropical rainforest from deforestation.

Since many of these large-scale measures are difficult for an individual to do, people can now purchase "carbon offsets", emission reduction credits from an organisation's project that results in less carbon dioxide or other greenhouse gases in the atmosphere. They are measured in tonnes of CO_2 equivalents (or

"CO_2e") and are bought and sold through a number of international brokers, online retailers and trading platforms. Whether you want to neutralise the carbon emissions of a single long-haul flight or your entire existence, offsetting personal emissions is easily done by visiting online retailers and using their calculators to determine the emissions related to the activity you want to offset. This is then translated into a fee that the company will use to soak up a matching amount of carbon.

Although offsetting is proving extremely popular among individuals, global corporations and celebrities, it has met with a lot of criticism too, as many of the offset projects do not make the swift carbon savings that they claim. Tree planting, for instance, was very popular in the past, but young trees can take decades to soak up the carbon you have paid to offset, which is one reason why many offsetting companies are moving towards more sustainable energy projects such as wind farms (see box), rainforest protection, methane capture from landfills or livestock and carbon sequestration projects that absorb carbon dioxide directly from the atmosphere.

Before making a commitment to a project, do your research to ensure that the offset project is certified and that you are getting the maximum benefit from your investment, rather than paying for the company's overheads. Clean Air-Cool Planet thoroughly evaluates key carbon offset retailers.

BECOMING CARBON NEUTRAL AND DECARBONISING The goal of reducing emissions and offsetting any unavoidable emissions is for an individual or an organisation to become carbon neutral, which means achieving zero net carbon emissions. While this admirable, there is an even better goal to aspire to. Becoming decarbonising or carbon positive is not just to break even, but to start removing additional carbon from the atmosphere—on top of that which you now produce—to attack climate change head-on and make a more substantial impact. This can be done by reaching ideal energy efficiency, offsetting unavoidable emissions and creating an oversupply of clean energy. The most important step when getting started is to determine what you can do on a daily basis to reduce your ecological footprint.

SIX SENSES CARBON OFFSET PROGRAMME IN CONJUNCTION WITH THE CONVERGING WORLD

Working with the non-profit organisation the Converging World, the Six Senses Carbon Offset Programme is designed to neutralise all carbon emissions related to Six Senses' resort and spa operations, including guests' flights. By 2010, Six Senses plans to be carbon neutral and to be decarbonising by 2020, and this will be achieved in part by replacing coal-fired power plants with Suzlon® wind turbines in India.

The Converging World generates clean energy in developing countries and profits go into renewable energy and community development. The organisation installed a 1.5-megawatt Six Senses wind turbine, large enough to provide energy to a small town (with approximately 5,000 residents) in Tamil Nadu. During its 20-year lifespan, the Six Senses wind turbine will generate approximately 80,000 megawatt-hours of clean, renewable electricity, averting the release of 70,000 tonnes of carbon into the atmosphere. Revenue from the electricity is split between local community projects, a "breeder fund" to replicate the model and investments in further carbon reduction strategies in other locations.

ECOLOGICAL FOOTPRINT The ecological
footprint is a measure of our consumption
levels in terms of the total area of the earth's
surface needed to support our individual
existence. This area, measured in hectares of
average productivity, is calculated around the
amount of land, fresh water and sea that is
needed to feed us. It also takes into account
the emissions generated from the oil, coal and
gas that we burn at ever-increasing rates, and
it determines how much land is required to
absorb our waste.

The World Wildlife Fund's Living Planet
Report (2006) estimated that only one-quarter
of the earth's surface is available to meet our
needs. One-quarter of the earth's surface
equals 11.3 billion hectares (27.9 billion acres),
which must be divided between just over six
billion inhabitants. Therefore, each person's
sustainable ecological footprint is only about
1.9 hectares (4.6 acres). The report also found
that the world's ecological footprint has tripled
since 1950. It highlighted that on a global
scale, we are consuming an amount of
resources in one year that takes an average of
one year and three months to replace.

Industrialised nations are the worst culprits,
with huge ecological footprints that reveal how
much more than their fair share of the earth's
resources they are squandering. Those
countries topping the list include the US (9.6
hectares or 23.7 acres per person), Canada
(7.6 hectares or 18.8 acres), Australia (6.6
hectares or 16.3 acres), France, Belgium and
the UK (5.6 hectares or 13.8 acres).

If everyone in the world lived as most
Europeans do, we would need three planets to
support us; the average North American
lifestyle requires the equivalent of five planets.
China, although currently at the one planet
level, has such a large population that if its
rapid development continues, its impact upon
the planet's natural resources is likely to
increase substantially.

For further information and to calculate
your personal ecological footprint, visit one of
the many available websites, such as
www.footprint.wwf.org.uk, www.footprint
network.org or www.zerofootprint.net. Once
you have taken stock of the size of your own
footprint, it becomes much easier to
implement effective changes.

CARBON CAPTURE AND STORAGE

Carbon capture and storage (CCS) is a concept based on capturing carbon dioxide from fossil fuel power plants in order to mitigate their carbon emissions. It has been estimated that CCS technology has the potential to trap up to 90 percent of the carbon dioxide emissions from power stations and industrial sites. CCS involves collecting, transporting and then sequestering (or burying) the carbon dioxide so that it does not enter the atmosphere and cause climate change.

The three main trapping techniques are: post-combustion CCS, which involves scrubbing the power plant's exhaust gas using specific chemicals; pre-combustion, which takes place before the fuel is placed in a furnace by first converting the fuel into a clean-burning gas and stripping out the carbon dioxide released by the process; and finally, oxyfuel, which involves burning fossil fuels in an atmosphere with high amounts of pure oxygen, resulting in a waste gas that is almost pure carbon dioxide. Once the carbon has been trapped, it is liquefied, transported and buried. However, the technology is costly with experts calculating that up to 40 percent of a station's energy could end up being used to run CCS, while retrofitting a station to handle CCS would cost millions of dollars.

CCS also has applications outside of the realm of power plants. For instance, biochar is charcoal created by pyrolysis (chemical decomposition from heating at high temperatures) of biomass (living and recently dead biological material). Agricultural and tree waste can be turned into biochar through a process that captures carbon dioxide. Then, the biochar can be buried (see box).

PYROLYSIS

Biomass

Charcoal

Carbon recycled by trees

Wood

Pyrolysis oven

Biochar sequestered in soil

The burning of trees and agricultural matter contributes a significant amount of carbon dioxide into the atmosphere. Biochar can potentially store this carbon in the soil for thousands of years. Also, its presence in the earth can improve water quality, increase soil fertility and raise agricultural productivity. Although current biochar projects are small and are making little impact on the overall global carbon budget, expansion of this technique has been advocated by experts.

Elements in the process of pyrolysis, which creates biochar. Biochar can store carbon that would otherwise be released into the atmosphere.
OPPOSITE: A coal-fuelled power station.

ENERGY When our ancestors first learned how to ignite a fire, they were developing a means of harnessing energy. Since then, we have used energy from burning wood, dung, coal, petroleum and natural gas and by using water, steam, wind and uranium. Fossil fuels are the primary energy souce today. Every year, at least one million years worth of fossil fuels are burned. This is a frantic rate that cannot be sustained. Moreover, it has been estimated that almost 65 percent of global warming is a direct result of the combustion of oil, coal and gas (Stern, World Resources Institute, 2006).

While individuals can reduce their energy consumption dramatically and make a substantial impact on carbon emissions, this in itself is not enough. To get more substantial reductions, experts agree that fossil fuels must be replaced by a renewable energy mix produced using a combination of solar energy, hydropower, wind power, geothermal energy and biofuels. Additionally, deforestation must be severely curtailed and emerging technologies such as carbon capture and storage (CCS) must be refined to reduce any remaining greenhouse gas emissions from the burning of fossil fuels.

Energy is central to almost all aspects of our lives, but its language varies tremendously. In the developed world, energy equates with speed, power and efficiency: petrol to run cars, electricity to power homes and computers to power work and education. In the developing world, energy can be as basic as survival: being able to boil water to prevent disease and death. Here, millions of people (mostly women and children) spend many hours a day collecting fuel for heating and cooking. If they have access to modern technology, they pay disproportionately high prices for it. In Africa, for example, according to IUCN's the World Conservation Union report "The Nature of Energy" (2007), almost 80 percent of the continent's rural population have no access to electricity. The majority of these people rely on burning traditional biomass such as wood and agricultural waste. While Africa has abundant renewable, clean energy sources, the technology remains inaccessible to the vast majority. However, if gaining access to energy can have such a profound effect on people's lives, why is it taking so long to rectify the current paradigm, especially when the technology is available?

Reducing our overall energy consumption and increasing the quantity of energy available is the challenge. Life on earth has changed energy forms twice before: first from wood to coal, and then from coal to petroleum. Each change took some 40 years to implement fully, and both changes were fraught with resistance.

Renewable energy—solar, wave, wind, biomass and geothermal—represents value, efficiency, safety and, ultimately, the best possible solution to the problems of climate change, energy needs and economic security. However, although the market for clean energy technology is becoming highly sophisticated, it cannot be ignored that the key to cost-effectively improving energy efficiency is to reduce overall consumption.

Installation of the deep sea water cooling pipe at Soneva Fushi by Six Senses, Maldives.
OPPOSITE: A villa at Soneva Fushi by Six Senses, Maldives, which is cooled by the energy-efficient deep sea water cooling system.

DEEP SEA WATER COOLING AT SONEVA FUSHI BY SIX SENSES

New technology that can reduce energy expenditure in homes is being developed and tested every day. Deep Sea Water Cooling (DSWC) is one example of cutting-edge technology, and it is currently in place at Soneva Fushi by Six Senses, Maldives. In situ since 2008, it supports the resort's commitment to zero-carbon energy by the end of 2010. It is the first of its kind to be installed in Asia, and through its implementation, further applications of this energy-saving technology are more likely.

The 3 km (2 miles) of 25 cm- (12 inch-) diameter, long-life plastic piping was assembled at sea. The pipe was laid to a depth of 300 m (328 yds) beneath the water, where the temperature is about 11°C (52°F) and spans the sea to reach a pump house on the island. From here, the cold water is directed through trenches to guest villas, where heat exchangers are used instead of energy-intensive air conditioning units. The result is efficient cooling that saves 70 percent of energy, in comparison to the energy required by standard systems.

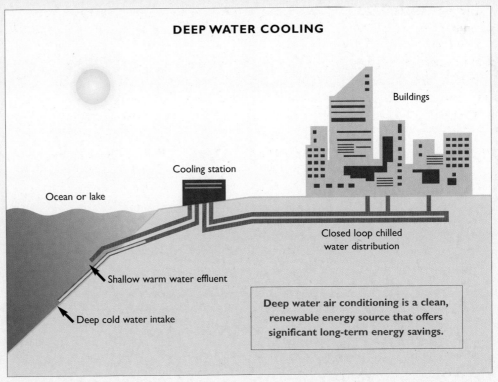

DEEP WATER COOLING

Buildings

Cooling station

Ocean or lake

Closed loop chilled water distribution

Shallow warm water effluent

Deep cold water intake

Deep water air conditioning is a clean, renewable energy source that offers significant long-term energy savings.

SOLAR ENERGY The sun gives over 10,000 times more energy than the world consumes. From this perspective, there is no energy problem. It is stationary, clean and practical, and it does not require fuel. However, it is the reliance on less sustainable forms of energy and the practicalities of using solar energy that are the issues. Also, while solar energy is technically viable, it is expensive to capture, store and derive high yields from, and as it is dependent on the amount of sun, it is highly variable and must be stored at a cost. What's more, large manufacturing plants are required to produce the photovoltaic (PV) cells needed to power solar energy on a bigger scale.

There are two kinds of solar power: solar energy, in which light is converted into energy (e.g. from solar PV panels) and solar thermal energy, in which heat from the sun is converted into energy.

- PV panels: These panels consist of two or more thin layers of semi-conducting materials that, when placed on a roof or outside wall (exposed to light), generate electrical charges which are conducted by direct current into the building's electricity supply. As the voltage generated from a single cell is low, many cells are connected to form a solar panel. More discreet forms of panels are now available such as solar slates that are designed to replace conventional roof tiles and can be both extremely neat and effective. While solar panels work year-round, a slight drawback for cooler climates is that there is a considerable difference in the energy generated between the summer and winter months.

- Solar thermal hot water panels: Roof-mounted solar thermal panels harness the sun's energy directly into heat. Although there are many systems available, the typical set up is a roof-mounted solar collector panel that channels the sun's energy into a hot water tank, which stores the heated water during the day so it can be used at night. It can be used for hot water or direct cooling through an absorption chiller. The collector is combined with a traditional water heating system or combi boiler (that heats water on demand) and can provide about 30 percent of an average household's hot water needs, thereby reducing the household's carbon emissions.

- Concentration solar power systems: These systems use lenses or mirrors and tracking systems to focus a large area of sunlight into a small beam. The concentrated light is then used as a heat source for a conventional power plant. Basically, there are two types: concentrating solar thermal (CST) and concentrating photovoltaics (CPV). CST is used to produce renewable heat or

Solar panels at Evason Phuket, Thailand.
OPPOSITE (FROM TOP): Biodiesel to run garden machines is produced at Evason Phuket, Thailand, from used cooking oil with this machine; elements in the process of making air conditioning from burning garden waste.

electricity. Although a large range of concentrating technologies exists, the most developed are the solar trough, parabolic dish and solar power tower. Each method is capable of producing high temperatures and correspondingly high thermodynamic efficiencies, but they vary in the way that they track the sun and focus light. With CPV systems, sunlight is concentrated onto PV surfaces to produce electricity. There are many types of solar concentrators available that are most often mounted on a solar tracker to keep the focal point on the cell. CPV operates most effectively in very sunny weather because clouds and overcast conditions create diffuse light that is not easily concentrated.

BIOFUEL Biofuel is solid, liquid or gaseous fuel derived from recently dead biological materials. It is easily distinguished from fossil fuels that are derived from biological matter that has been dead for a long time (often millions of years). Biofuel systems vary dramatically in complexity from a stand-alone stove that will heat a single room to a wood-pellet, chip or log boiler that can heat water and also run an entire central heating system.

For domestic use, non-wood biomass such as animal waste, biodegradable products and high-energy cereal grains can be used as fuel. Domestic biomass is a far more energy-efficient and a significantly cheaper alternative to electricity, liquid petroleum, gas and oil, and although it is not entirely clean (as it pumps some carbon dioxide into the atmosphere), it still prevents up to 7 tonnes of carbon dioxide from being released into the atmosphere per year, compared with the more polluting electricity generated by fossil fuels.

Garden waste

Garden waste burned in furnace boiler

BIOMASS ABSORPTION CHILLER AT EVASON PHUKET & SIX SENSES SPA, THAILAND

The biomass absorption chiller is the first commercial application of its kind installed in Thailand. It converts the heat produced by burning garden waste to air conditioning that is used to cool the shipping and receiving building at Evason Phuket & Six Senses Spa.

The biomass absorption chiller is expected to burn approximately 250 kg (550 lb) of garden waste per day to create 20 tonnes of air conditioning, which is enough to cool a 600-sq-m (6,458-sq-ft) storage building 24 hours per day.

The biomass stoker has a combustion efficiency of 97 percent. Additionally, the process is renewable and results in zero carbon emissions, because as foliage like branches and leaves fall to the ground, new growth replaces them and mops up any carbon released.

This experimental project is a joint venture between the Energy Maintenance Service (Phuket, Thailand) and KSM-Stoker (Denmark) and is supported by DANIDA (Danish International Development Agency), under the Danish Ministry of Foreign Affairs.

Absorption chiller converts heat to chilled water

Air conditioning

Geothermal power plant in Grindavík, Iceland.
OPPOSITE (FROM TOP): Hydroelectric power plant, Niagara Falls, Ontario; the Green School in Bali, Indonesia, generates hydropower using cutting-edge vortex technology.

GEOTHERMAL POWER Ground source heat pumps or geothermal exchange systems extract latent heat from the ground via a borehole or network of underground pipes. The system is ideally suited to a new home, where the pipes can be buried underneath the structure, or to an existing house with garden space. The heat is transferred to a mix of water and antifreeze and then converted via the heat pump into thermal energy for heating the home and water.

While electricity is needed to power the pump, it is estimated that the electricity used will amount to only one-third of the total energy produced by the system. The pump can also be powered by solar energy or another form of renewable energy, which would limit carbon emissions even further.

COMBINED HEAT AND POWER (CHP) CHP technology captures and uses the heat generated when fuel is burned to produce electricity. Micro-CHP units replace the conventional boiler in a home central-heating system with a small gas engine that drives an electrical generator which powers domestic lights and appliances. The waste heat from the engine heats both rooms and water. CHP can reduce carbon emissions and energy consumption by about 25 percent. Homes fitted with CHP can remain connected to the electricity grid to retain back-up boilers and ensure that they are never short of energy.

HEAT RECOVERY SYSTEMS Domestic heat recovery systems are generally used to reduce the energy required to heat a home in the winter and cool it in the summer. Typically, they consist of two separate air handling units: one that collects and exhausts stale air from the inside of a building; and one that draws in fresh air and distributes it through the home. Both air systems pass through a heat transfer module, and although they remain physically separate, heat from the exhaust air is transferred to the fresh incoming air.

HYDROPOWER Hydropower is derived from the force of moving water, which generates electricity through the turning of turbines. Hydropower can be produced by harnessing the power of waves and tides and by using water wheels and hydroelectric dams. It is a viable and cost-effective option anywhere there is moving water.

Micro hydro is the domestic version that is most suited to those living close to a river or stream or in an area close to a disused water mill. Water flowing downhill over a natural waterfall or man-made weir is diverted via a pipe through an enclosed turbine that rotates to produce electricity. After leaving the turbine, the water is discharged back into the river. Micro hydro can be a reliable energy option, but the amount of power produced is directly dependent on the height that the water falls from and the volume of water that passes through the turbine.

WIND POWER Wind turbines use the force of the wind to rotate aerodynamic blades and create electricity. Most small domestic wind turbines generate direct current (DC) electricity and require a battery and inverter to convert this current into alternating current (AC) electricity. If the system is connected to a national grid, this conversion will happen automatically. Domestic wind turbines are relatively cheap and easy to install. However,

they are dependent on the speed of the wind and are, therefore, unpredictable. Also, they may kill birds and should not be placed along their migratory paths.

HYDROGEN POWER Hydrogen is the most abundant element in the universe and a potent energy source. NASA uses hydrogen to launch space shuttles into space, companies such as Boeing are pursuing hydrogen as a cleaner fuel option and hydrogen-driven buses are currently in experimental use in some large cities. Hydrogen is plentiful, clean and portable. Unfortunately, however, the fuel cells are fragile and costly to produce, and a lot of energy is required to separate the hydrogen and oxygen in water. Further research is required in order for hydrogen to become a viable energy source.

WATER Although two-thirds of our planet is covered in water, less than 3 percent of it is fresh, with less than 1 percent available for human consumption. Of this tiny amount, 20 percent is estimated to be too remote for human access and much of the rest is not collected for use. So, the fresh water we rely on is rare, for such an essential natural resource (World Water Commission, 2000).

Since approximately 70 percent of the human body is comprised of water, an ongoing intake is needed for almost every bodily function, from breathing to lubricating the joints and eliminating toxins. While we can survive weeks without food, deprived of water, the body cannot survive more than a few days. The World Health Organization (WHO) says that while individual water needs depend on age, gender, health, levels of physical activity and quality of diet, the average adult should drink about 2 to 3 litres (4 to 6 pints) of water per day, the average child about 1 litre (2 pints).

DOING THE MATH: WHY NOT TO DRINK WATER BOTTLED IN PLASTIC*

- 1,500 plastic water bottles end up as rubbish every second.
- In 2004, 26 billion litres (55 billion pints) of bottled water were purchased. This equates to approximately 28 billion plastic bottles, of which 86 percent ended up as rubbish.
- To produce these bottles, 17 million barrels of oil were used. This quantity of oil could have fuelled 100,000 cars for one year.
- US$100 billion are spent by consumers every year on bottled water and recent research suggests that for a fraction of this cost, everyone around the world could have safe drinking water and effective sanitation.

* According to the Earth Policy Institute (EPI).

SPARKLING OR STILL?

Six Senses makes its own Six Senses Drinking Water produced to the highest international drinking water standards. It is processed on-site at each of the group's resorts. The water is purified in a reverse osmosis plant, using a three-stage filtration method and ultraviolet light. The water is remineralised, and aeration is added to create the sparkling style. It is bottled only in glass and sealed with an airtight rubber and ceramic stopper that is clipped in place with a metal clasp. Although glass may be a costlier alternative, it is reusable and prevents the crossover contamination that has been associated with some plastic bottles.

Some years ago, bottled mineral water became trendy for its supposed medicinal and cleansing benefits. This market escalated rapidly. Between 1994 and 2002, the global bottled water market grew by almost 250 percent (www.sustainweb.org). In the UK alone, between 2000 and 2005, there was an estimated 10 million new bottled water drinkers. To satisfy this thirsty market, the water is not only wrapped in plastic but also transported often enormous distances around the planet before being drunk, and then the bottle is thrown away. Every step of the way, energy is consumed. While many plastic bottles can be either reused or recycled, unfortunately, the great majority end up in landfills. On top of this is the fact that many of these bottled waters come from a source that can be up to 16,000 km (10,000 miles) from their final destination.

Once a bottle is empty, further resources are expended when sending it for recycling, making each bottle's footprint even larger.

Tap water is by and large the best option for the planet. To ensure it is safe enough to drink, there are a number of filter options on the market, from jug filters containing activated carbon, ion exchange resins that reduce heavy metals and plumbed-in systems that treat water through a separate two-way tap.

An increasing number of more ethical bottled water brands are appearing on the market. These donate some or all of their profits to charities working to improve access to water in poor countries. Many use only recycled and biodegradable bottles. While these initiatives may lead to an improvement of some of the disconcerting statistics, they still cannot match the environmental benefits of tap water.

FROM LEFT: Evason Phuket, Thailand, is self-sufficient in terms of water for its guests, staff and garden. The aerator at the waste water treatment plant is part of the process, ensuring that no waste is released into the ocean and no fresh water is used for garden irrigation; bottled drinking water is produced by Six Senses at each resort.
OPPOSITE: Used plastic bottles heaped incredibly high at a recycling mill.

FROM TOP: Composting of food and garden waste is done at all Six Senses resorts; Eco Centro at Soneva Fushi, a waste recycling and food production centre.
OPPOSITE (FROM TOP): Gardens thrive when compost is added to soil; cardboard boxes covered with mulch or compost degrade into earth and help form nutrient-rich soil.

WASTE

Fifty years ago, almost all of what we consumed was produced close to our homes. Today, even the simplest purchases like water or an apple can come from thousands of miles away, wrapped in substantial amounts of packaging that is destined to end up as waste in a landfill.

Despite growing concerns, many of the products we buy are non-biodegradable, and with the world's population living closer and closer together, waste has become a very serious environmental issue. As noted in *Ready, Set, Green Eight Weeks to Modern Eco-Living* by Graham Hill and Meaghan O'Neill, the average US citizen is estimated to produce about 2 kg (4 lb) of rubbish every day, while a citizen of Germany or Sweden by contrast will generate less then 0.9 kg (2 lb) per day.

In many countries, this waste is very poorly managed, without landfills or government-driven recycling schemes. The Thai island of Phuket, for example, must rely on burning waste in incinerators and private recycling initiatives. With the municipal incinerator able to burn only 250 tonnes of waste per day, half of the daily 500 tonnes of waste produced is sent to the landfill that is located right next to a mangrove forest. During heavy rain, toxins leach out into the sea.

With smaller average households, increased reliance on convenience foods and higher food hygiene standards, packaging represents a growing share of the average household's waste, as these factors encourage the use of disposable packaging and individual portions. Added to this is the fact that packaging in international trade is a major marketing tool—a vector for brand names and consumer values. The manufacture of packaging generates waste after a particularly short lifespan. Think about it. We buy a CD, container of food or bar of chocolate, unwrap the plastic and throw it in the bin before even benefiting from the goods inside. A single plastic bag from the supermarket might be used for 20 minutes, but can take up to 500 years to degrade in a landfill. The UN's Environment Programme estimates that globally we go through 16,000 plastic bags per second (www.grida.no/publications/vg/waste2/). They are given away in huge quantities by grocery stores and supermarkets all over the world. Most of these bags are not biodegradable and end up in dumps or polluting landscapes. This waste can be immediately reduced if consumers make the effort and bring their own bags.

When everyday items such as plastic, paper, containers and food remains end up in the dump, they either decompose, releasing methane (a greenhouse gas about 20 times more potent that carbon dioxide) or they are incinerated, which releases carbon into the atmosphere. Degradation occurs very slowly. Even readily biodegradable items such as vegetable cuttings can remain in landfills for many years due to a lack of oxygen. All the more reason to reduce, reuse and recycle—in that order, as follows:

- Reduce—Buy only what is absolutely required and nothing more.
- Reuse items as much as possible.
- Recycle items only after their usable lifespan is definitely complete.

Also, battery disposal is responsible for a large portion of the release of toxic heavy metals. In 1996, the use of mercury was phased out in batteries, and proper recycling methods began, along with required labelling that included disposal information. Although

BIOMIMICRY AND CRADLE-TO-CRADLE

Nature represents the ultimate waste-free, closed-loop system. In the science of biomimicry, scientists look to nature to solve human problems by creating materials that are strong and functional but that return to a natural state once we are done with them.

Cradle-to-Cradle is a holistic economic, industrial and social framework that seeks to create systems that are not just efficient but essentially waste free. In the current model developed by Michael Braungart's team at the Environmental Protection Encouragement Agency, all materials used in industrial or commercial processes are categorised as either technical or biological nutrients.

Technical nutrients are non-toxic, non-harmful synthetic materials with no negative effects on the natural environment. They can be used in continuous cycles as the same product instead of being downcycled into waste. Biological nutrients are organic materials that once used will decompose into the soil, providing food for small life forms without affecting the natural environment. The success of this system will depend on the ecology of the region; for example, organic material from one area may be harmful to the ecology of another country or landmass. However, the possibilities offered by this research are encouraging.

REDUCE—REUSE—RECYCLE AT SIX SENSES

Every effort is made to reduce the amount of waste generated at Six Senses Resorts & Spas by making responsible purchases, in particular, limiting non-biodegradable products such as plastic. Where possible, most products purchased companywide are biodegradable or natural. Natural rubbish bags are used, and suppliers are asked to reduce packaging and deliver to all resorts in bulk. In countries such as the Maldives, that is home to Soneva Fushi and Soneva Gili, Six Senses works with local islands as well as organisations to tackle waste issues, which are likely to become even more of a problem if sustainable waste management policies and practices are not adopted throughout the islands.

Other companywide waste management initiatives include:

- Refillable ceramic containers for soap, shampoo, conditioner and body lotion are used instead of disposable, plastic ones.
- Recycled paper is available in all guest rooms.
- Guests are provided with complimentary Six Senses still or sparkling water, produced on site, in reusable glass bottles.
- No plastic bags are issued to either staff or guests, and no plastic items of any kind are given to guests.
- Waste separation operates in all resorts but is dependent on national recycling facilities.
- The composting system converts organic food and garden waste into fertile soil for use in the herb and vegetable gardens.
- Guests are requested to take home used batteries and other potentially toxic waste.

At Soneva Gili by Six Senses, Maldives, tea lights made from recycled glass bottles create a nice atmosphere. OPPOSITE: A table designed from cement and recycled glass at Soneva Fushi by Six Senses, Maldives.

rechargeable batteries contain heavy metals such as nickel-cadmium, they are preferable to the single-use version. Rechargeable batteries should be disposed of carefully. The same applies to other household hazardous waste such as paint, paint thinners, cleaners, oils and pesticides—all of which should be disposed of according to municipal guidelines.

PLASTIC Plastic pervades our lives. Enormous amounts are used every year to store food, drinks, personal care products, medicines and more. It has been estimated that a staggering 17 million barrels of oil were used to produce 28 million plastic bottles in the US in 2006 alone (www.earth911.com).

There are at least seven types of plastic that are used on a regular basis, some sturdier than others, some safer for your health or for the environment and some best avoided.

The number stamped at the bottom of a plastic container represents the type of resin made to produce the plastic. Because each resin is different, these numbers affect how and where plastics can be recycled and identify its associated risks and recycling potential. The majority of plastic types can be recycled, but in terms of numbering, the most significant issue is correctly identifying and sorting each plastic item, as this is crucial in the recycling process. Mixed plastics cannot be effectively recycled.

Also, health concerns surround the use of plastics. A number of petroleum-based chemicals are used in the manufacture of plastics. Some leach into food and drinks and can potentially have an impact on human health. Leaching increases when plastic is scratched or comes in contact with oily or fatty foods during heating and when exposed to sunlight. Certain detergents will also degrade plastic, allowing the chemicals to leach out. The plastics most commonly associated with leaching are polycarbonate, PVC and styrene. However, this does not imply that other plastics are entirely safe.

BIOPLASTIC Bioplastics are made of biopolymers, derived from renewable biomass sources such as vegetable oil and cornstarch. Made from naturally-derived ingredients, they are essentially biodegradable, a major selling point separating them from petroleum-based plastics. Due to these environmental credentials, they are becoming a popular packaging option for major retailers (see www.earth911.com/plastic).

Polylactide plastic (PLA) is a bio-based plastic derived from sugar or starch feedstock that is fast gaining popularity for bottles, service ware, wrappers, films, containers and textiles. PLA is a thermoplastic and can be mechanically ground and reused. However, due to its low commercial volume, it cannot as yet be recycled in the conventional way, but the excellent news is that it will decompose in roughly two weeks in a compost heap, in comparison to most plastics, which take up to 100 years to biodegrade. There are no known human or ecological health concerns associated with the use or disposal of PLA (see www.sustainablepackaging.org).

TYPES OF PLASTIC

Number/Name: **#1 Polyethylene terephthalate (PET or PETE)**
Where is it found?: Single-use water bottles; soft drinks and juices; liquid cough medicine.
Is it safe?: Yes, although there is some risk of chemicals leaking into product. Water bottles should only be used once.
Easy to recycle?: Yes.

Number/Name: **#2 High density polyethylene (HDP)**
Where is it found?: Bleach, detergent and shampoo bottles; translucent milk bottles; some plastic bags.
Is it safe?: Yes, although there is some potential risk of chemicals leaking into product.
Easy to recycle?: Yes.

Number/Name: **#3 Polyvinyl chloride (PVC)**
Where is it found?: Meat wrappers; cooking oil bottles; some water bottles; some detergent and window cleaner bottles.
Is it safe?: Questionable, because PVC contains phthalates that are suspected carcinogens and hormone disruptors.
Easy to recycle?: Yes, but make sure to separate #3 plastic from #1 plastic. Mixing them can disrupt the recycling process.

Number/Name: **#4 Low density polyethylene (LDP)**
Where is it found?: Shopping bags; sandwich bags; cling wrap; paper towel wrappers; opaque reusable baby bottles.
Is it safe?: Yes, although there is some risk of chemicals leaking into product.
Easy to recycle?: Yes, but not all recycling programmes accept LDP.

Number/Name: **#5 Polypropylene (PP)**
Where is it found?: Yoghurt pots; straws; clouded containers; some baby bottles and disposable nappies.
Is it safe?: Yes, there are no known risks associated with PP.
Easy to recycle?: Not all recycling programmes accept PP.

Number/Name: **#6 Polystyrene (PS, Styrofoam)**
Where is it found?: Disposable cups; disposable cutlery; Styrofoam takeaway containers; CD jackets.
Is it safe?: Questionable, as both the clear form and the more common Styrofoam contain styrene, a suspected carcinogen and hormone disruptor that can leach into food.
Easy to recycle?: Many recycling programmes do not accept PS.

Number/Name: **#7 Polycarbonate (PC)**
Where is it found?: Most baby bottles; sippy teething cups; water bottles; water cooler bottles; food storage; metal food can liners; medicine bottles.
Is it safe?: Questionable, as PC contains bisphenol A (BPA), a suspected carcinogen and hormone disruptor. Do not heat PC plastic. BPA-free baby bottles are now available.
Easy to recycle?: Many recycling programmes do not accept PC.

- See www.ewg.org for more information.

LOCAL KNOWLEDGE: THE SPECIES THAT SHARE OUR WORLD

The earth we abuse and the living things we kill will, in the end, take their revenge; for in exploiting their presence we are diminishing our future.

- Marya Mannes, More in Anger

Animals in their habitats are one of nature's greatest gifts. Places such as Nepal's Sagarmatha National Park, the marine profusion of Australia's Great Barrier Reef, the Asiatic forests spanning Thailand, Laos, Cambodia and Vietnam are all areas of superb biodiversity and truly irreplaceable sources of life and inspiration. However, the bleak reality is that if temperatures and sea levels continue to rise and severe droughts persist, the many animal and plant species on earth face a very grim future, threatened not only by the devastating effects of climate change, but also by disappearing habitats and relentless hunting and fishing.

Think about it: the Arctic without the polar bear and Africa without the elephant. If the Tibetan antelope becomes extinct, nothing will bring it back to life. These are depressing thoughts, but we must consider the very real possibility that these events could occur in our lifetimes. According to the UN, species are becoming extinct 100 times faster than the rate shown in fossil records. The IUCN estimates that a total of 15,000 plant species are threatened by extinction. This figure represents only 2 percent of the world's documented plants, hinting at the awe-inspiring variety of nature that human activity is threatening. Yet, as only about 4 percent of the world's plants have been evaluated, the true percentage of threatened plant species is expected to be much higher.

Animals and plants have evolved over thousands of years to live in specific environments, but climate change is happening quickly, leaving them unable to adapt. However, there is hope as many species once named as endangered have been rehabilitated by human action. For instance, after much concerted effort, the majestic bald eagle, teetering on the edge of extinction since the 1970s, is no longer considered endangered. With awareness and decisive action, we can begin to undo past damage and prevent further destruction.

Clownfish and sharks cohabitating in the Maldivian waters.
OPPOSITE: The pristine atolls of the Maldives.
PREVIOUS: A black bear wanders through a meadow dotted with fallen trees in Yellowstone National Park, Wyoming, US.

Snorkeller amidst a school of fish in the Maldives.
OPPOSITE (FROM TOP): Increased temperatures and the corresponding droughts can cause habitats to become dry wastelands; illegally-traded elephant tusks on display.

THE FIGHT AGAINST EXTINCTION

Many organisations, both governmental and NGOs, work tirelessly to safeguard the future of the celebrated and vulnerable symbols of our biodiversity. Among these are the WWF (www.worldwildlife.org), Freeland (www.free-land.org); TRAFFIC, the wildlife trade monitoring network (www.traffic.org); the IUCN (www.iucn.org); the Conference of the Parties to CITES, the Convention on International Trade in Endangered Species of Wild Fauna and Flora (www.cites.org); the UN (www.united

nations.org); BirdLife International Partnership (www.birdlife.org) and the Phoenix Fund, an NGO that protects the fauna and flora of the Russian Far East (www.phoenix.vl.ru).

According to the 2008 IUCN Red List of Threatened Species, widely recognised as the most authoritative assessment of the global status of natural species, more than 16,000 animal and plant species are now threatened with extinction. Scientists warn that even our closest relatives, the great apes, could be extinct in just 20 years.

The ultimate cause of stress for so many different animal species is that many habitats are quickly disappearing, and there are near-constant emissions of various toxic pollutants into ecosystems. In addition to these threats, many species must also struggle to survive in the face of excessive hunting and unfamiliar weather and temperature patterns. Sensitive ecosystems are suffering from soil loss and degradation, ground water depletion and the accumulation of toxins.

It is believed that the influence of humans on the natural world has reached a level that no other species has ever achieved in such an oppressive manner and over such a short period of time in the history of life on earth. In many parts of the world, complete forests have been stripped, while wetlands and rivers have been over-exploited and polluted, all of which has altered the delicate natural balance that is vital to life on earth.

SUCCESS STORIES Species can be, and have already been, saved from extinction. However, it is far more effective and economical to protect a habitat in the first place than to try to restore it or to attempt to reintroduce a species into the wild.

EXTINCTION

The IUCN says extinction is a natural process. According to fossil records, no species has yet proved immortal. But the rapid loss of species we are seeing today is estimated to be between 1,000 and 10,000 times higher than the expected natural extinction rate. And unlike the mass extinction events of geological history, the current phenomenon is one for which a single species—human beings—appears to be almost wholly responsible.

Several species including the Chinese crested ibis, Mauritius kestrel, Hawaiian goose, white rhino and short-tailed albatross have all moved down the IUCN Red List threat categories or have been removed from the list all together, offering a few success stories that prove the positive impact that humans can make. A combination of measures, including the enforcement of legislation that protects species and habitats; education of local communities; limiting the use of pesticides, herbicides and other chemical pollutants; and captive breeding and reintroduction programmes, all helped to spark this recovery.

The destiny of endangered species depends on us. While governments and NGOs around the world are doing their utmost to redress the imbalance, it is up to us to rethink our relentless exploitation of natural resources and help preserve the lives of these truly remarkable and irreplaceable species.

BIODIVERSITY Biodiversity or biological diversity is the term given to the total variety and complexity of interactions of all life on earth. The biodiversity we see today is the result of billions of years of evolution, shaped by a combination of natural processes and, increasingly, by human influence.

Biodiversity is integral to the effective functioning of ecosystems. The rapidly escalating loss of biodiversity has widespread implications for both human and environmental security. The monetary value alone of goods and services provided by ecosystems is estimated to amount to some US$33 trillion per year—nearly twice the global production resulting from human activities. About 100 million tonnes of aquatic organisms, including fish, molluscs and crustaceans, are

Higher temperatures and dry land will lead to an increased prevalence of blazing forest fires.
OPPOSITE: Pollution affects human habitats as well, making it difficult to breath in some cities.

taken from the wild every year, and these species represent an essential contribution to world food security.

DEFORESTATION Trees are unique. They are like individual factories that fervently consume carbon dioxide to produce food energy and oxygen through photosynthesis. They are often referred to as the "lungs of the earth", as they sink carbon and provide oxygen for the rest of the planet. Forests are also important for preventing soil erosion, flooding and landslides. Also, as trees extract groundwater through their roots and release it in the atmosphere, they are important to the planet's fresh water resources. Tropical rainforests are estimated to produce

30 percent of the world's fresh water. Tropical forests occupy about one-third of earth's land area and are home to more than half of the world's terrestrial species. What's more, they have existed some 45 million years; they have survived the test of time.

However, today, in many parts of the world, nature's oxygen-producing machines have been sacrificed to satisfy the demand for raw materials and energy. Agriculture, timber production and oil palm plantations are some of the biggest culprits, and unless we work to preserve what remains of the rainforests, they may no longer be around to feed us our life-supporting oxygen.

So severe is the crisis that the Food and Agriculture Organization (FAO) of the UN estimates that annual net loss of forest cover is about 7.3 million hectares (18 million acres). For example, it is anticipated that only about 10 percent of the original forests remain in Madagascar, and every one of the 31 primate species that these forests support is now endangered. The local communities who once lived at one with their environment, using the forest's resources to meet their needs, face dire consequences from the world's insatiable demand for cheap timber.

Deforestation is estimated to account for about 20 percent of the world's carbon emissions. A mechanism suggested for tackling climate change has been the idea of using "carbon sinks" to soak up carbon dioxide. Reforestation, or the planting of new forests, has been suggested as a method for creating these sinks. While there may be some potential in this solution, it is criticised primarily because it legitimises the continued destruction of old growth that is an established biodiversity base. New forest area means the creation of entire ecosystems. It is also denounced for being a quick fix that does not tackle the root cause of the current problem and does not lead to or promote actual emission reduction.

The FAO 2009 "State of the World's Forests" report found that the health of the world's forests varied from region to region. Although advances are being made in places such as Europe and developed areas in Asia, the forest situation in Africa presents big challenges, reflecting the additional hurdles that must be overcome when implementing conservation measures in areas ridden with poverty and inadequately developed institutions.

The report warned that the demand for wood is expected to rise, primarily because of an increase in its use as a source of renewable energy. Further, the potential for large-scale commercial production of cellulosic biofuel will have an unprecedented negative impact on the world's forests, most notably in countries like Indonesia, where many natural forests are being razed to make way for palm plantations and biofuel production. Although the development of this renewable energy source seems positive at first glance, many biologists warn there is simply not enough land on the planet to feed the growing number of hungry people and to grow fuel.

Man tending his beehive.
OPPOSITE (FROM TOP): A tiny
newborn panda nestled in
blankets in an incubator;
a display of sharks' fins that
are used for sharks' fin soup.

ANIMALS AT RISK: ON LAND

The number of species at risk are too numerous to list here, but the following are examples of some of the planet's most endangered terrestrial species. This small sampling hints at just how pervasive the problem has become and how much we have to lose if it continues:

BEES (ANTHOPHILA): Albert Einstein is believed to have predicted that when the bee population dies, the death of the human race would soon follow. As whole colonies have already been wiped out in many parts of the world, his hypothesis may indeed be on track.

It has been estimated that at least one-quarter of the 2.5 million honeybee colonies in the US have been mysteriously wiped out in recent years. Colony collapse disorder (CCD), where hives are found suddenly deserted, leaving only queens, eggs and a few immature workers, has increased in frequency. While researchers have not as yet determined the exact cause of CCD, they have found that pollution is making life more difficult for bees and other insects. Pollution is believed to dramatically reduce the distance the scent of flowers can travel, making it increasingly challenging for bees to locate them, thereby preventing bees from pollinating them. Other experts say that radiation from mobile phones is interfering with the bees' navigation systems and preventing them from finding their way back to their hives.

Regardless of the exact cause, bees are vital for biodiversity. More than 130,000 plants depend on them for pollination. If taken to the extreme, in a world without enough bees, crops and fodder could become impossible to cultivate, threatening the survival of produce, livestock and hence the human race.

GIANT PANDA (*AILUROPODA MELANOLEUCA*): Having once ranged throughout most of southern and eastern China, the giant panda is now confined to the mountainous bamboo forests found in the provinces of Sichuan, Shaanxi and Gansu in southwestern China.

The greatest threat to this precious species is a restricted and degraded habitat, a result of thousands of years of cultivation and clearing of bamboo for agriculture (pandas spend over half of their day feeding on more than 60 species of bamboo).

Although poaching was a serious problem in the past, it has diminished greatly as penalties for poaching became far more severe and the market for panda skins has virtually disappeared. Concerted efforts are now being made in China to increase both the quality and quantity of the panda's habitat, with forest reserves developed specifically for the conservation of this venerated animal.

BROWN BEAR (*URSUS ARCTOS*): Once the most revered and powerful predators in Europe, with the densest and most immense pan-European forested hunting ground imaginable, today, much of the brown bears' playground has disappeared, leaving the species confined to small protected forest areas, generally lacking in food supplies.

A combination of the fragmentation of its natural environment from deforestation and agriculture, poaching and accidental killing during wild boar hunts has put this bear further at risk. Its population is extremely reduced, and its future rests entirely on us. Experts have warned that we either take a step backwards to guarantee a habitat for the bear or accept its disappearance forever.

PREVENTING SPECIES LOSS
BY STEVE GALSTER

Steve Galster is founder and director of Freeland, an environmental and human rights organisation based in Bangkok, Thailand. He is Chief of Party for ASEAN-WEN Support Program (Association of Southeast Asian Nations Wildlife Enforcement Network) and presenter of the Crime Scene Wild series on Animal Planet International. He shares his thoughts on species loss and his work to prevent it as follows:

"When we hear scary statistics about species extinction rates around the world, it's hard to relate that back to our everyday lives, where most of us are unlikely to notice wild species at all.

I've been working to reverse the decline of species loss since 1991 when I started conducting undercover investigations, tracing the poaching of endangered wildlife from the forest and oceans to the organised crime groups running the trade, whose impact has made wildlife crime the third most profitable form of black market commerce in the world, behind drugs and guns. I have found myself inside a warehouse stuffed with the remains of 520 dead rhinos, stockpiled by a mafia group banking on the African and Asian rhino's extinction. As a phoney 'buyer' I have been given access to many secret stockpiles, which included tiger skins, sharks' fins, whale meat and Tibetan antelope fur among others, all being prepared for distribution to wealthy buyers.

The human race has pushed many wild animals back into pockets of untrawled waters and deep into what's left of our forests. Consequently, habitats have been left deserted and degraded, without the invisible inputs of these diverse creatures. While most of us are aware of the dangers of global warming and the importance of planting trees and keeping our waters clean, we must remember that wildlife is the blood of every healthy ecosystem. A forest or ocean without a diverse and robust population of wild animals and plants will soon become a dead forest or sea. The solution is more than just stopping deforestation and reducing pollution; it's allowing life to return to our forests and oceans. To rewrite this story, I founded Freeland, an environmental and human rights group. We work with communities, governments and partner organisations to raise public awareness, while beefing up protection for species under threat through organised crime. Consumer awareness has been a key to our successes to date. Back in 2001, for example, we launched a campaign to stop people from buying sharks' fin soup. This prompted a dramatic drop in sharks' fin consumption in Bangkok and a multi-million dollar lawsuit by sharks' fin restaurant owners trying to silence my team. By raising awareness for the plight of other animals, we have reduced the prevalence of poaching of Siberian tigers and arrested the world's largest rhino horn mafia in China.

To help us achieve our goals and stop the destruction, the onus is on the consumer to be more aware of how their purchases are impacting ecosystems and livelihoods elsewhere. It can be as simple as asking a market vendor, furniture store or restaurant owner where a product comes from. If travelling, do your research and question tour operators about where animals have come from and how they are cared for; or avoid tourism activities involving captive wildlife altogether.

Your enquiries affect the market because you are the market. For me, being an aware and responsible consumer is an important part of carving out a sustainable and compassionate life."
- Steve Galster (www.free-land.org)

A polar bear lies sedated in the snow as US Geological Survey researchers take samples to determine the health of the dwindling polar bear population in Kaktovik, Alaska.
OPPOSITE (FROM TOP) The rare and beautiful Iberian lynx; snow leopards at home in the mountainous plains of central Asia.

POLAR BEAR (URSUS MARITIMUS):

To many, the image of the downy white polar bear trapped on a small floating iceberg in search of food has become one of the most disturbing images of the impact of climate change on the world. With experts forecasting that the polar ice cap will disappear almost entirely during the summer months within the next 100 years, the largest predator in the Arctic marine ecosystem faces a very uncertain future—so much so that the IUCN predicts that of the 19 populations of polar bears that inhabit the Arctic (in Canada, Alaska, Russia, Norway and Greenland), five will go from a "high risk" to "very high risk" of decline within the next decade.

The world's 20,000 to 25,000 polar bears have adapted to live in a highly specialised manner, in order to survive in the ice-covered waters of the circumpolar Arctic. Their low rates of reproduction, combined with their long generational spans, make their adaptation to rapid habitat changes unlikely. Further, certain areas of the Arctic have very high levels of pollutants. Being the apex predator of the food chain, polar bears are exposed to these loads that can have a detrimental effect on their immune systems, growth patterns, reproduction and overall survival rates.

The primary challenge facing the bears, of course, is the disappearing ice. Those with continuous access to ice can hunt throughout the year; however, in areas where the ice already melts during the summer, the bears are forced to spend several months on land, fasting on stored fat reserves and being exposed to poachers until the freeze-up recommences. With the diminishing size of the

ice pack, bears now have less and less time available to obtain food, and when the ice begins to melt and break off into the ocean, the bears become floating prisoners on ice.

IBERIAN LYNX (*LYNX PARDINUS*): This European feline is twice the size of the domestic cat and one of the rarest cats in the world. At the end of the 1980s, its population numbered about 1,100, distributed throughout Spain and Portugal. Today, its estimated population totals less than 150, scattered throughout areas of southwestern Spain.

Because of its narrow habitat and its dependence on the wild rabbit as prey, the lynx is naturally vulnerable. The dramatic decline in rabbit populations, as a result of disease and habitat change, has had a direct impact on its numbers. Massive conservation intervention is currently underway to reverse their decline. Captive breeding programmes have been established where the captive-bred animals are later released into the wild. However, despite these initiatives, current numbers are not sufficient for the species to survive in the long term, and experts agree that this feral cat is on the brink of extinction.

SUMATRAN TIGER (*PANTHERA TIGRIS SUMATRAE*): Of the eight known subspecies of tigers, only five remain. Of these, the Sumatran tiger, the largest of the big cats, is believed to be most at risk of extinction.

Once found throughout an area stretching from the Caspian Sea to the Indonesian island of Bali, today, between 400 and a few thousand of these elusive hunters remain scattered through the Sumatran forests of Indonesia. These forests face the continuous threat of deforestation, and only small isolated pockets remain for the tiger to call home. Also,

poaching continues for its pelt, bones and other organs that are used in traditional Asian medicines, making the outlook for the tiger appear very grim.

SNOW LEOPARD (*UNCIA UNCIA*): Home for the shy and reserved snow leopard lies in the bleakest and most hostile regions of the planet—the vast mountainous plains of central Asia (from Afghanistan, Bhutan, China, India, Kazakhstan, Kyrgyzstan, Mongolia, Nepal and Pakistan to Russia, Tajikistan and Uzbekistan). The animal is well adapted to survive at very high altitudes with its thick dense fur, enlarged nasal and chest capacity to aid breathing and its long, heavy tail that helps maintain balance in motion and body warmth.

Snow leopards are indicated on the IUCN's Red List as endangered, as they are suspected to have declined by at least 20 percent over the past two generations, with an estimated 7,500 specimens remaining. The main threats to its survival include habitat and prey loss, conflict with locals, illegal trade for their bones (used as a substitute for tiger bones in traditional Chinese medicine) and hides (six to 12 hides will make one fur coat). The snow leopard is now protected in almost all of the countries throughout its range, and the sale of its fur and body parts is prohibited by international law. However, it still suffers persecution and illegal poaching, primarily as a result of a lack of awareness.

TIBETAN ANTELOPE (*PANTHOLOPS HODGSONII*): The Tibetan antelope or *chiru* is at home at altitudes of more than 5,000 m (16,400 ft) over the Chinese high plains (with a small population migrating towards the Ladakh region of India). Their extraordinarily light, warm down fur allows them to survive on a freezing

plateau. *Shahtoosh*, a Persian word meaning "king's wool", is the name given to the shawls woven primarily in Kashmir from this very delicate down hair. For hundreds of years, these shawls were part of the dowry that each Kashmiri girl brought into marriage—a tradition that did not endanger the antelope until these shawls were discovered by the Western world.

The hair from up to five antelopes is required to make one *shahtoosh* shawl. To meet the demand for *shahtoosh*, about 20,000 antelope are illegally massacred every year, and their skinned carcasses and bones are abandoned on the Tibetan plateau steppe. Although international trading in *shahtoosh* is banned, illegal hunting and selling continues, especially in Tibet, where the enforcement of the law over such a vast area of habitat has proven to be very problematic.

ELEPHANTS (*ELEPHANTIDAE*): Elephants have populated the earth for five million years. Their only surviving representatives are the Indian/Asian elephant and the African. Because elephants require much larger areas of natural habitat than most other terrestrial mammals, they are among the first to suffer the consequences of habitat fragmentation and destruction. They face other threats too, including poaching for the illegal ivory trade and human-elephant conflicts, through which hundreds of humans and elephants die every year. As their ultimate survival outside protected areas is inextricably linked to integration with humans, mitigating these conflicts has become one of the largest conservation challenges today. Conservation experts stress the importance of educating local cultures to value elephants as economic assets from which they can benefit.

- African elephant (*Loxodonta africana*): One of the most powerful symbols of African wildlife, this elephant is the largest living land mammal and present in 37 countries in sub-Saharan Africa. A distinctive feature of African elephants is their enormous ears that span up 3 m (10 ft) in length and their ivory tusks. During the 1970s, the population was estimated at around 1.3 million, and currently it is believed to be less than 470,000.

- Asian/Indian elephant (*Elephas maximus*): It is estimated that only about 30,000–35,000 Asian elephants remain in the wild, living primarily in Bangladesh, India, Sri Lanka and parts of Nepal, Indonesia and Thailand. Another 15,000 or so can be found in captivity (in circuses, zoos and doing commercial deforestation work). As only the males have tusks, their needless and abject slaughter for the ivory trade has caused drastic demographic alterations in some parts of Asia, with only one adult male remaining per 100 females.

ORANGUTAN (HOMINIDAE): The largest arboreal mammals on earth today, orangutans are native to Indonesia and Malaysia. Today they can be found only in rainforests on the islands of Borneo (Bornean orangutan, *Pongo pygmaeus*) and Sumatra (Sumatran orangutan, *Pongo abelii*). Best described as the "gardeners of the forest", they play a vital role in seed dispersal, especially for larger seeds that are not easily dispersed by smaller animals. For 40,000 years, the orangutan has managed to co-exist with humans, sharing the wealth of tropical forests. But ruthless hunting for trophy collections, combined with a decline in forests, has left the species struggling to survive. The Sumatran orangutan is regarded as critically endangered by the IUCN, with an estimated decline in numbers of more than 80 percent in the last 75 years. The decline persists as forests within its habitat continue to disappear at alarming rates.

GIBBONS (HYLOBATIDAE): Gibbons are tree monkeys that live in the tropical rainforests of southeast Asia. These light, agile animals spend their lives suspended from branches, picking fruits from the highest layers of the forest. Of the 14 species of gibbon, half are now at risk of extinction, the most notable being the indigenous Javan silvery gibbons (*Hylobates moloch*) and the black crested

gibbons (*Nomascus concolor*), which are spread throughout the forests of Vietnam and Laos. Hence, without doubt, the greatest threat to their survival is deforestation, driven by the demand for timber and intense oil palm cultivation. Added to these serious threats is the illegal removal of live specimens for the lucrative international market, as well as a growing demand for their organs, which are highly valued in traditional medicine.

RHINOCEROS (RHINOCEROTIDAE): What once numbered in the hundreds of thousands now amounts to only a few thousand, with just five main rhino species surviving in the world today: the Indian or Asian rhinoceros (*Rhinocerus unicornis*), the Javan rhinoceros (*Rhinoceros sondaicus*), the Sumatran rhinoceros (*Dicerorhinus sumatrensis*), the African black rhinoceros (*Diceros bicornis*) and the African white rhinoceros (*Ceratotherium simum*).

The main threats to their survival are habitat loss and poaching for the international rhino horn trade, where high prices are paid for their horns, which are used to make ornately carved handles for the ceremonial daggers worn in some Middle Eastern countries.

FROM TOP: A Sumatran tiger cub cuddles a young female orangutan for extra warmth at the Taman Safari Indonesia Animal Hospital, as both have been rejected by their mothers;
a baby rhinoceros in the elephant park located in Nairobi, Kenya.
OPPOSITE: Herd of African elephants grazing at dusk in Botswana, Africa.

ANIMALS AT RISK: IN THE SEA

For a long time, the sheer expanse of the oceans (covering over 70 percent of the planet's surface) and the land-bound existence of humans meant that marine ecosystems were left relatively undisturbed. Very little was known about them. A lasting legacy of this fact is that only 1 percent of the oceans are protected, compared to 12 percent of the land surface. In the past, human beings used inefficient fishing techniques that were limited to coastal areas, crudely exploiting a fraction of the seas and leaving the bulk of marine habitats untouched.

This scene has changed radically over the last 100 years with the advent of intensive fishing; rising sea levels; the dumping of chemicals, pesticides and refuse from agricultural and industrial waste; and the discharge from petroleum tankers, all of which are altering the delicate physiochemical balances, food chains and biodiversity of the seas and are ultimately jeopardising the continued existence of many species. The only viable solution is the rapid implementation of sustainable fishing practices on a global scale to ensure that humane and sustainable fishing becomes the norm, rather than the exception.

The following selection of animals represents a small percentage of the species in our seas that face an uncertain future:

BLUE WHALE (BALAENOPTERA MUSCULUS): The largest animal ever observed, the blue whale can reach lengths of more than 30 m (100 ft) and weigh more than 30 elephants. The blue whale is found in all oceans except the Arctic. During the last century, as a result of whale hunting, it almost became extinct, but since 1967, it has been protected. Now the population is estimated to be between 2,500 and 5,000. The main threat to its existence is still direct human exploitation.

FIN WHALE (BALAENOPTERA PHYSALUS): Nicknamed the "greyhound of the ocean" because of its speed, the fin whale is the second largest animal in the world. Prior to the advent of modern whaling in the late 19th century, fin whales were largely immune to human predation because they were too difficult to catch. Formerly one of the most common whales on the planet, the global population has declined by more than 70 percent over the last three generations, due primarily to commercial whaling.

SHARKS (CHONDRICHTHYES): There are approximately 1,200 recognised shark species that have adapted themselves to ecosystems around the world. Sharks are integral to these systems as they maintain the health of fish populations, regulating their numbers and reducing the spread of disease. A decline in shark numbers can lead to an increase in fish numbers, which in turn can cause a crash in the populations of small marine life that the fish feed on, such as plankton. Therefore, without sharks, an entire ecosystem can become endangered, and unfortunately, many shark species have been classified as such on the IUCN's Red List.

Sharks are hunted for sport, but they are most commonly killed for commercial finning (sharks' fin is a delicacy in greater China). The shark-finning procedure involves cutting off the fins and then throwing the dying bodies back into the sea. Although finning has been banned in some countries, millions of sharks still face a painful death every year as a result of this cruel market.

We ourselves feel that what we are doing is just a drop in the ocean. But the ocean would be less because of that missing drop.

- Mother Teresa

FROM TOP: Sharks maintain the health of entire oceanic ecosystems by regulating the size of fish populations; sharks, after being de-finned, are thrown back into the sea, unable to survive.
OPPOSITE: As a result of hunting by whalers, the blue whale was pushed to near extinction, but now, after dedicated conservation measures, the species is making a comeback.

CORAL

(CNIDARIA)

The word coral conjures images of pristine waters and colourful reefs within snorkelling distance of the shore. However, much more than just a picturesque setting, tropical corals are among the most studied and revered ecosystems on earth.

Each individual coral animal is called a polyp, and most live in groups of hundreds to thousands of genetically identical polyps, which form a colony. Coral are generally classified as either hard or soft coral. There are around 800 known species of hard coral, also known as the reef-building corals. Soft corals, such as sea fans, sea feathers and sea whips, live in colonies resembling brightly coloured plants and are found in oceans from the equator to the north and south poles. Soft corals also generally live in caves or on ledges where they can easily capture food floating by in the currents.

Coral reefs are created by millions of tiny polyps forming large carbonate structures that are home to thousands of other species. They are the largest living structure on the planet and are often called the "rainforests of the sea", due to the vast amount of species they harbour. The reefs have evolved on earth over the past 200 to 300 million years, and over this evolutionary period, their most unique feature is undoubtedly their highly evolved form of symbiosis. Inside the tissues of each coral polyp live tiny microscopic single-celled plants, known as zooxanthellae, that share space, gases and nutrients to survive. This symbiotic relationship contributes to the brilliant colours of coral that can be seen while diving or snorkelling.

Covering less than 1 percent of the ocean floor, reefs support an estimated 25 percent of all marine life, with over 4,000 species of fish alone. Coral reefs provide economic and environmental benefits to millions of people. They offer coastal protection from waves and storms and are sources of food, pharmaceuticals and jobs. However, according to a 2008 report produced by the Global Coral Reef Monitoring Network (GCRMN) and supported by the IUCN, the world has lost about one-fifth of its corals, and many of the remaining reefs could die in the next 20 to 40 years unless humans reduce greenhouse gas emissions (see www.gcrmn.org).

Scientists concur that climate change is the biggest threat to reefs. As emissions of carbon dioxide increase, oceans absorb more of the gas and become more acidic, damaging a wide range of marine life, including coral, plankton, lobsters and sea grasses, among others. In addition to this, rising sea surface temperatures are resulting in the phenomenon of coral bleaching. This is a stress response by the coral host that occurs when the symbiosis between corals and zooxanthellae breaks down, resulting in the loss of the symbionts and a rapid whitening of the coral host. If the temperature decreases, the stressed coral can recover; if it persists, the affected colony can die. These climate-induced threats are strengthened by other negative factors, such as over-fishing, destructive fishing methods that use dynamite and cyanide, pollution and coastal development.

Humans are instigating major reef recovery operations, especially in areas such as Australia's Great Barrier Reef, the Indian Ocean and the western Pacific. However, while having a positive impact, these measures cannot fully combat the continual onslaught of warming seas.

FROM TOP: Tropical coral reefs nurture an effervescence of colourful life forms; sea fans are a type of soft coral, which undulate gently in the currents.
OPPOSITE: The Great Barrier Reef, the largest coral reef system in the world.

SEA TURTLES (*CHELONIOIDEA*):

Sea turtles have inhabited the earth for more than 150 million years. Unlike many other marine reptiles, they never separated completely from the dry land to which they still return to lay their eggs. Turtle population numbers are believed to have decreased by over 95 percent in recent years. This reduction is occurring primarily in the coastal areas of developing countries, where the direct collection of turtle eggs or removal of specimens for food carried on unabated until

relatively recently. Litter causes chaos too. Plastic bags are a serious threat, as turtles mistake them for jellyfish and swallow them. The bags get caught in their digestive systems, causing the turtles to starve.

Currently, only seven species of sea turtles remain. Among these are the most commonly sighted and endangered loggerhead turtle (*Caretta caretta*), which lives either in deep sea environments or in shallow sea beds near the coast. The hawksbill turtle (*Eretmochelys imbricata*) is critically endangered, with an estimated 87 percent decline in numbers of mature females nesting annually (over the last three hawksbill generations).

This unfortunate fate is the combined result of exploitation of the adult female and her eggs, nesting sites being damaged or destroyed and humans hunting for ornamental turtle shells. Today, as a result of conservation efforts, some protected populations are reported to be increasing in numbers, especially in the Caribbean.

For instance, the Caribbean Conservation Corporation (CCC) is a not-for-profit organisation based in Florida, US. CCC is one of the oldest and most accomplished sea turtle organisations in the world, and since its inception in 1959, its work has greatly improved the chances of survival for several species of sea turtles. Also, CCC offers ways for everyone to get involved, by providing a calendar of worldwide events that informs the public about opportunities like observing hatchlings being released into the wild (see www.cccturtle.org).
SOUTH ASIAN BOX TURTLE (*CUORA AMBOINENSIS*): The South Asian box turtle is threatened with extinction, with a TRAFFIC report stating that unregulated trade (up to 100 times the legal level) has led to the disappearance of the turtle from parts of Indonesia. The turtles are used for meat and in traditional Chinese medicine, with major markets in Hong Kong, China, Singapore and Malaysia, almost all of which are primarily supplied by Indonesia. The animals are also exported as pets to the US and Europe. The report found at least 18 traders operating illegally throughout Indonesia, trading more than two million turtles per year, with the vast majority destined for export.

ANIMALS AT RISK: IN THE AIR

According to BirdLife International, the natural rate of bird extinction is one bird species per century. However, in the last 30 years alone, 21 bird species have become extinct. At present, 190 are classified as "critically endangered". These birds are the rarest of the rare. They are on the brink of extinction, and without some kind of immediate conservation action, many will not be here in 10 years.

The primary reason for the extremely rapid disappearance of many species of birds is the destruction of habitat from deforestation. Birds, too, are suffering the fate of many other rare animals—ending up as prized trophies by hunters who have their kills stuffed and exhibited in the home or sold on the international market. BirdLife International says that to compound the problem, acid rain has caused the population decline of several bird species that breed in the eastern US, in particular. Despite clean-air legislation, many regions of North America continue to have acid rain, with a number of bird species experiencing rapid population declines.

However, for many of these species, conservation action is well underway. Initiatives include education, media campaigns, the establishment of guidelines for sustainable tourism, the creation of protected forests, close monitoring of the cage bird trade and a ban on the trafficking of many bird species.

The following are examples of critically endangered birds, as listed by BirdLife International on behalf of IUCN:
PHILIPPINE EAGLE (*PITHECOPHAGA JEFFERYI*): The Philippine islands of Mindanao, Luzon, Samar and Leyte are home to one of the largest eagles on the planet, the

Police discover baby birds being sold illegally in Bangkok, Thailand.
OPPOSITE: Moken tribesman swims to catch a turtle, a traditional source of food for the tribe, in the Mergui Archipelago, in the Andaman Sea, Myanmar.

Philippine eagle. With a wingspan of almost 2 m (7 ft) and a head wreathed in a crown of feathers, it is one of the most endangered animals on the planet. Now, only about 250 survive in the wild.

HYACINTH MACAW (*ANODORHYNCHUS HYACINTHINUS*): This stunning cobalt blue bird is one of 23 species of macaw, and among the largest and rarest parrots in the world. The blue feathers were traditionally used by indigenous tribes for decoration, which led to the large-scale capture of up to 10,000 birds for sale on the international market. Currently, only three populations remain, all in Brazil. They have been protected since 1987, and as a result of conservation programmes, some populations have even increased in numbers. But the illegal removal of the young from nests continues to threaten the survival of the species.

BLUE-THROATED MACAW (*ARA GLAUCOGULARIS*): This rare macaw is confined to the Beni region of northern Bolivia, where the wild population was discovered in 1992. Its population is believed to have declined rapidly since its discovery, principally as a result of illegal exploitation for the cage bird trade. All known habitats occur on private cattle ranches, where clearing to make pastures and tree-felling for fuel has reduced the number of suitable trees for nesting and has inhibited the regeneration of the Motacú palm (*Attalea phalerata*), its principal food source. Research conducted in 2007 estimated that the total population numbers only between 250 to 300.

WHITE-SHOULDERED IBIS (*PSEUDIBIS DAVISONI*): Home for this graceful ibis is Cambodia, Vietnam, Laos and East Kalimantan, Indonesia. Its population has declined dramatically during the 20th century, and it has been described as the most threatened large water bird in southeast Asia. The species has a severely fragmented population (numbering fewer than 250 mature individuals), as a result of deforestation, drainage of wetlands, hunting and disturbance. Its population is projected to decline by over 80 percent during the next three generations or 25 years.

Western Siem Pang, Cambodia, is the most important site for the species, where 108 birds were recorded in November 2006. The government there has made a commitment in principle to designate the area a "protected forest", but it is currently threatened by plans for a plantation concession, which would result in large-scale forest clearance, extensive road development and immigration into the area.

PLANTS AT RISK
More than 70,000 species of plants are used medicinally all over the world. Throughout much of human history, medicinal plant species have simultaneously been treasured and taken for granted. They have been freely available and used as a basic resource for treating the ills of countless generations, originally within Asia, and later throughout much of the rest of the world. With the present shrinking of wild habitats, definitive changes in current collection and trade practices will be required if medicinal plants are to survive in the wild and continue to be available for use by future generations.

The following are examples of medicinal plants appearing on the IUCN's Red List of threatened plant species:

ARNICA MONTANA (DAISY FAMILY):
Arnica montana is also known as leopard's bane, wolf's bane and mountain arnica. It is a European high-alpine flowering plant with a tall stem and large yellow capitula. It grows in nutrient-poor siliceous meadows. Overall, it is rare, but it can be locally abundant. However, it is becoming even rarer, largely due to intensive agricultural practices that are wiping it out. It is widely used in homeopathic creams for strains, sprains, bruising and trauma. Used topically, arnica preparations have been shown to act as effective anti-inflammatory agents that assist in healing. However, if taken internally in large amounts, the plant can also be poisonous to humans.

DALBERGIA NIGRA (LEGUME FAMILY):
Often referred to as Brazilian rosewood, this legume species rates among the most highly prized woods in Brazil. It grows in the rich soils of hygrophilous forests. The timber has been harvested since colonial times for high quality furniture, flooring and musical instruments. The wood's rate of regeneration is poor, and with the rise in deforestation, it is now both endangered and illegal to trade. Brazilian rosewood essential oil is widely used in perfumery (e.g. Chanel No. 5).

PANAX QUINQUEFOLIUS (IVY FAMILY):
Panax quinquefolius, commonly known as American ginseng, is an herbaceous perennial that is routinely used in Chinese and Native American medicine in order to stimulate the body's vital energy.

The herb is native to eastern North America, but it is also grown commercially in the US and China. As a result of its popularity in traditional medicines, the plant has been over-harvested and is now rarely seen in the wild in most parts of the US.

PRUNUS AFRICANA (ROSE FAMILY):
Known as red stinkwood, this evergreen tree is native to the montane regions of sub-Saharan Africa and the islands of Madagascar, San Tomé, Fernando Po and Grande Comore. The mature tree is 10 to 25 m (30 to 80 ft) in height, open-branched, and it is often pendulous in forests. Although it is listed as vulnerable in the IUCN Red List, some experts say that as long as some montane forests survive somewhere within its enormous range, the tree is not in any major danger of extinction.

Besides deforestation, the greatest threat to it is the harvesting of its bark in an unsustainable manner. Many trees have died as a result of girdling, caused by bark removal. Its bark is a renowned herbal therapy for prostate problems and is exported worldwide.

SLOW FOOD
an organic feast

SLOW FOOD: AN ORGANIC FEAST

How and what we eat determines to a great extent the use we make of the world—and what is to become of it. To eat with a fuller consciousness of all that is at stake might sound like a burden, but in practice few things in life can afford quite as much pleasure.

- Michael Pollan, *The Omnivore's Dilemma*

Just 20 years ago, luscious red strawberries were undoubtedly some of the best summer treats imaginable. Today, soulless varieties appear on winter plates, and winter's best greens are on year-round display on supermarket shelves. Times have changed, and we have in a relatively short period of time industrialised our entire food chain—a change that is in contradiction to the laws of nature. Mother Nature did not plan for strawberries to be plentiful during harsh winter months, when they could not be at their sweetest. The resources required to ship food across the world, the pesticides and genetic alterations that allow fruits and vegetables to grow in inhospitable conditions and the preservatives used to make food last have all taken a toll on our health and the environment.

Nor did Mother Nature foresee how many of her animals and fish would live and die for human greed. From shark-finning and drift net fishing to calves being reared in crates and fed specialised liquid diets through tubes, relentless and inhumane practices have exploited the natural world.

As Carol Petrini, founder of the Slow Food movement, states, "Food production at a global level is today one of the most unsustainable human activities. Agriculture and industrial food transformation have plundered nature, impoverished soils, polluted water and air." However, it might not be too late to let Mother Nature become our inspiration for a more sustainable and wholesome way of living.

First, we must examine our relationship to food. Is it something to be cherished or merely something to sate our hunger? The food of convenience—filled with preservatives and artificial flavourings—eaten on the run has drained the simple pleasure of eating, of enjoying a leisurely meal with family and friends, of revelling in the joy of seasonal, freshly prepared meals. To preserve the real taste of food and the heart-warming enjoyment that goes with it, we must adopt a SLOW way of eating, living more thoughtfully and carefully on the planet that feeds us.

This driftwood table centrepiece, filled with attractive and edible morning glory, makes beautiful, practical use of a material that would normally be discarded. OPPOSITE: Showcasing fresh local ingredients, the delicious spa cuisine at Six Senses Destination Spa-Phuket features dishes such as grilled red emperor on Thai sweet potato with ginger glaze. PREVIOUS: The Fresh in the Garden restaurant at Soneva Fushi by Six Senses, Maldives, allows guests to enjoy fresh organic food, while surrounded by a lovely natural setting.

The landscaping of Six Senses Destination Spa-Phuket is made up of edible plants, such as lemongrass, morning glory and banana trees, providing ingredients that often appear on the resort's food menu.
OPPOSITE (FROM TOP): Watering the lettuce at the organic vegetable garden of Evason Phuket, Thailand; sun-ripened cherry tomatoes are full of vitamins and antioxidants that can help prevent cancer.

WHY EAT SLOW? With today's mass-market consumption, the taste and nutritional value of many foods have been damaged by techniques of convenience. Methods for improving shelf life, increasing yield, guaranteeing hygiene and promoting the year-round availability of produce are often achieved by modifying the food to a "new and better" model with more potential for commercial success. But in most cases, this model strips the food of its natural goodness and has a negative impact on the planet.

Those who have started to question how their food choices affect their families and the world can be left uncertain as to what to eat. What should you buy: an organic apple grown in another country or a local apple grown down the road? Should I support the farmer who employs exclusively biodynamic principles and techniques even if the produce must be transported across the world before ending up on my plate? So many diverse questions with one unifying answer—of course, it should be the food that tastes the best and brings the most unashamed pleasure to eat. Our purchasing power can have a dramatic impact on how food is produced and the types available, and by making conscientious choices that take into account local and organic principles along with taste, we can support deserving farmers and companies.

As consumers become increasingly discerning, searching in greater numbers for cleaner, purer food, the paradigm is finally starting to shift, as past traditions are being unearthed for a new and better way of eating. Dining is becoming less about bland uninspiring produce made more appetising with unhealthy additives and more about the heart-warming unadulterated goodness of real wholesome food. Much of this is due to the success of the Slow Food movement (www.slowfood.it). This movement seeks to protect invaluable food heritage in a world where the pleasures of taste are not always learned through leisurely meals around a lively table. It links the pleasure of eating with awareness and responsibility, believing that the enjoyment of excellent foods and wines should be combined with efforts to save countless traditional foods such as the cheeses, grains, vegetables, fruits and animal breeds that are disappearing due to the prevalence of convenient "fast" foods.

Eating Sustainable, Local, Organic and Wholesome (SLOW) food is less about topping up the body's energy levels and much more about arousing emotional satisfaction. It is about learning to taste, smell and adore even the simplest of fresh seasonal food, such as the ripeness of a freshly picked summer tomato or the newness of a richly green salad leaf. It is about living and being as you were born to by getting in tune with your body and the world

around you. It is about sparing a moment for those involved in the preparation of food, the farmers and the person who cooked the food for you, while you rediscover the joys of sharing deliciously fresh, soul-nourishing meals.

ORGANIC Organic agriculture is defined as "an ecological production management system that promotes and enhances biodiversity, biological cycles and soil biological activity". While most organic foods taste great and are packed with nutritional goodness, in recent years, the term has been abused for commercial advantage. Although organic practices cannot ensure that produce is completely free from residue (the difference between an organic and non-organic product might be minimal), the methods of production aim to minimise the pollution of the air, soil and water. However, in many countries, the control of organic production is not very efficient, which, when coupled with the insufficient knowledge of some food producers, causes the food not to be truly organic. In addition, many of the organically labelled fruits and vegetables on sale today were grown so far away that, by the time they get to your kitchen, they will have lost much of their goodness. Further, becoming certified organic is a costly and time-consuming process for small producers who often cannot justify the hefty price tag attached.

If buying organic, ensure that your local retailer can justify the higher price tag associated with most of the produce by asking where the product was grown, when it was picked and if it truly is organic. If you are satisfied with the response, you will be more certain that what you are buying is really doing you and your family some good.

THE SLOW FOOD MOVEMENT: A COMMENTARY

"The intellectual scope that Slow Food wants to bring into the gastronomy world is to renew gastronomic science itself, by treating it as a real science, multi-disciplinary and complex. If, as Jean-Anthleme Brillat-Savarin used to say, gastronomy 'refers to all that's inherent to the man as he feeds himself', then we have to consider a much wider range of fields of knowledge and human culture, compared with the sphere between folklore, elitism and recipes where for many years gastronomy has been banished.

Food production at a global level is today one of the most unsustainable human activities. Agriculture and industrial food transformation have plundered nature, impoverished soils, polluted water and air. Big inequities are persisting between different world populations—when every one of them could really have, whether they be poor or rich, the opportunity of exerting their own food sovereignty—and food quality and diversity have worsened.

To close oneself in a golden and elitist world made of gastronomic excellencies that few can afford, while the global food system is going adrift, would be stupid. It is also true that food should give us pleasure. But this should be the pleasure of eating everyday healthy food, seasonal food, local food, cooked in accordance with each person's culture, produced and distributed in a way that won't jeopardise earth and mankind's balance.

It is a difficult battle, which can be won only at a local level, implementing local modern economies that create a network with others. These local groups must be able to guarantee a food Good for those who eat it, Clean for the Earth and Fair for men that grow it. This is not utopia and not even a return to an ancient world. Traditional knowledge is important, just as the more modern is important: what is missing is a dialogue between the two sections.

Let's begin to see food with all the interconnections that it has with our lives and those of others; let's start to ask ourselves its origin, how much its production has polluted the environment and if someone has been exploited. Let's put food back to the centre of our lives; let's see it again as a systemic element, crucial for our wellbeing.

Life, just like food, is more complex and beautiful than how consumerism's fathers are presenting it. We need to find the strength to change, maybe by starting from our plates."
- Carlo Petrini, founder of the Slow Food movement

LOCAL AND WHOLESOME While the organic market continues to grow, according to many food purists, "local" is the new ideal that promises a healthier body and an even healthier planet. What's more, it is cheaper and, most importantly, smells and tastes like fresh, seasonal food should. It makes sense that a snow pea grown by a local farmer and that has never been near a refrigerator and has not accumulated a load of carbon miles from being shipped across the world will retain more of its delicate leguminous flavour and will be better for the environment than an organic snowpea that has been in a crate for weeks.

Choosing the best local produce in season means you can enjoy the best in taste as well as heart-healthy goodness.

Inseparable from local, wholesome foods are those eaten when at their most nutritious and tastiest—that means in season, free from chemical processing and as close as possible to where they were grown. As a result, none of their goodness is lost in trying to preserve the foods and in transporting them great distances.
FAIR TRADE The fair trade model is based on partnership and mutual cooperation that aims to improve the livelihoods of poor and marginalised workers in the developing world.

FROM TOP: Raw food salad of papaya and avocado, presented in a coconut shell, at Six Senses Destination Spa-Phuket; fresh local lettuce at the organic vegetable gardens of Six Senses Hideaway Hua Hin, Thailand.
OPPOSITE (FROM TOP): Freshly caught squid being dried by a local fisherman in Hua Hin, Thailand.

By encouraging long-term partnerships between the producer and the buyer, the fair trade system delivers more to farmers and workers than financial benefits alone. For many producers, fair trade can represent the difference between simply surviving and having the ability to invest in their present and make a plan for their future. With increased global spending on fair trade products, the Fairtrade Foundation in the UK estimates that over 1.5 million producers and workers in 58 developing countries now benefit from fair trade sales (www.fairtrade.org.uk).

TRADING FAIRLY

"Fair trade is a trading partnership, based on dialogue, transparency and respect, which seeks greater equity in international trade. It contributes to sustainable development by offering better trading conditions to, and securing the rights of, marginalised producers and workers...

Fair trade organisations (backed by consumers) are engaged actively in supporting producers, awareness raising and in campaigning for changes in the rules and practices of conventional international trade."

- FINE

For more information, investigate the very promising work being done and the important changes being made to promote the ideals of fair trade by the following **FINE** network of international organisations:

- Fair Trade Labelling Organisation International (www.fairtrade.net)
- International Federation for Alternative Trade (www.ifat.org)
- Network of European World Shops (www.worldshops.org)
- European Fair Trade Association (www.eftafairtrades.org)

THE GARDENS AT SONEVA FUSHI
BY SIX SENSES, MALDIVES

About half of the fruits and vegetables used in the kitchens of Soneva Fushi by Six Senses, Maldives, are grown and harvested in two organic gardens where the vegetable boxes are carefully plotted to ensure optimum crop production.

The fruit garden is designed around permaculture principles; therefore, the garden's own waste is used to make a rich compost that is later used in the garden to stimulate future growth.

Overlooking this tremendous green landscape is the resort's organic Fresh in the Garden restaurant that serves deliciously authentic menus created exclusively on **SLOW** principles. As it is impossible to grow all the ingredients required in situ, some fresh produce, most dried foods, oils, seasonings and vinegars are imported, but these foods are selected only if they are produced and transported in a sustainable manner.

Many of the wines served in the resort are specifically chosen from vineyards run according to organic or biodynamic principles. The wines are selected from passionate wine makers, creating a wine list for true connoisseurs.

FROM TOP: The interior of Fresh in the Garden; ripe mangoes ready to be picked from the organic garden at Soneva Fushi by Six Senses, Maldives.
OPPOSITE: Many dining tables of the organic Fresh in the Garden restaurant overlook the magnificent gardens of Soneva Fushi by Six Senses, Maldives.

THE GARDENS AT SIX SENSES HIDEAWAY HUA HIN AND EVASON HUA HIN, THAILAND

The gardens at Six Senses Hideaway and Evason Hua Hin, Thailand, grow an eclectic range of herbs, vegetables, fruits and mushrooms.

The entire garden is based on biodynamic principles, which have been adapted to the local environment under the guidance of experienced local farmers. For instance, the resort produces abalone mushrooms in an on-site mushroom hut, and these mushrooms are grown with the close involvement of the local community.

The gardens have their own wastewater recycling system that reuses water and filters waste through the garden's lakes, using the cleaner water for irrigation. As with other Six Senses resorts, an in-built composting system recycles leftover foods and other biodegradable waste into garden feed, which both reduces the waste that the resort must dispose of and enriches the soil to create thriving gardens.

Plans are in place for a new cooking facility, a children's sprouting garden, an educational workshop for the local community and a tea garden.

RAW FOOD The raw food diet consists of unprocessed and uncooked plant foods, such as fresh fruit and vegetables, sprouts, seeds, nuts, grains, beans, dried fruit and seaweed. Typically, at least 75 percent of the diet must comprise raw foods, in which the textures and ingredients of food are balanced with the goal of nourishing the body, mind and spirit. The rationale behind eating raw is that cooking food is thought to diminish the nutritional value and "life force" of the food. It is believed that cooking food above 42°C (108°F) destroys essential enzymes that assist in the digestion and absorption of food.

Proponents of raw food claim numerous benefits, including increased energy levels, easier digestion, weight loss and a reduced risk of heart disease, diabetes and cancer.

THE RAW CUISINE PHILOSOPHY OF SIX SENSES DESTINATION SPA-PHUKET

Clean, fresh, raw and natural is the mission of the kitchens of the Six Senses Destination Spa-Phuket on Naka Island. Almost everything that grows on the resort can be eaten, from the fruits and vegetables in the organic vegetable gardens to the lemongrass and basil in the private gardens of the guests' villas.

Where possible, organically grown produce is the first choice. All sprouting seeds and grains are grown on-site and harvested directly for use in the dishes served by the resort.

An exclusively raw menu is available for guests that prefer to enjoy the health benefits of food that is not subjected to heat over 42°C (108°F). Key raw food ingredients include nut milks, soya, almond, beans, pulses, sauces based on miso, yoghurt, olive oil, vegetable purees and tahini. Only raw oils like flaxseed, olive, grape and cold-pressed local oils are used.

CLOCKWISE FROM TOP: Wheatgrass growing at Evason Phuket, Thailand; mushroom hut at Evason Hua Hin, Thailand; raw mango and rambutan "cheeze cake".
OPPOSITE (FROM TOP): Garden planters can be made from recycled glass bottles; gardener at Evason Hua Hin with freshly picked produce.

La Raia's picturesque vineyards in Italy are run according to exclusively biodynamic principles. OPPOSITE (FROM TOP): Organic and biodynamic wines are becoming readily available; no heavy tools or artificial fertilisers are used to cultivate biodynamic vines.

BIODYNAMIC FARMING In 1924, Rudolf Steiner (1861–1925) presented a series of seminal lectures on "the spiritual foundations for a renewal of agriculture", in response to farmers' concerns about the depletion of soils and a general deterioration of crops and livestock that was due in part to the rapid introduction of chemical fertilisers. Biodynamics—the healing, nurturing, holistic, ecological, organic and spiritual approach to the sustainable care of the earth—was the result. Steiner was a respected scientific, literary and philosophical scholar, particularly known for his work on Goethe's scientific writings. His multi-faceted genius has led to innovative and holistic approaches to medicine, philosophy, religion, education, economics, agriculture, science, architecture and the arts.

Biodynamic farming is the oldest form of organic farming, which is enjoying a much needed revival in today's often toxic environment. Biodynamic methods consider the farm or garden to be a self-contained organism embedded in the living landscape of the earth, which is in turn part of a living, dynamic cosmos of vital, spiritual energies. Hence, the farm is thought to be a sustainable, self-contained organism. In practice, these ideas translate to creating a farm in which the health and wellbeing of the soil, upon which the success of the farm depends, is nurtured through crop rotations, manuring and pasturage. Care is taken not to have excessive output from the farm and, where possible, to keep the farm's produce self-contained. For example, land dedicated to the cultivation of

cow fodder feeds cows, whose manure can be used to enhance the overall fertility of the soil and hence the farm itself.

According to the biodynamic thought process, the quality of produce results from the quality of the environment: nature yields its most vibrant, flavourful fruit when farmed using a pure holistic practice, one that is completely in tune with the seasons and stars and maintains a healthy ecosystem in which insects and disease are naturally kept at bay.

THE BIODYNAMIC VINEYARDS OF LA RAIA, ITALY A fantastic example of the biodynamic principles at work, La Raia is a 100-hectare (250-acre) biodynamic farm comprising more than 28 hectares (70 acres) of gently sloping vineyards, grazing pastures and arable land about one hour from Milan. Through the tender nurturing of viticulturists Tom and Cateria Rossi Cairo, La Raia is producing top-quality biodynamic wines. The farm's rich clay limestone lies at around 400 m (1,300 ft) above sea level, existing in the perfect environment for the cultivation of the indigenous Cortese and Barbera grapes.

La Raia's year works in perfect tune with nature, and the complex relationship between climate, vine, roots and soil is carefully managed to ensure flavoursome grapes for wine making. Much of the work is performed manually following the vine's schedule, adding new vitality to the soil, which in the past had suffered from the use of heavy tools and tractors. Through this approach, genuine quality, Demeter-certified wine is produced. La Raia is also home to beef cattle, cereal and legume production, and a variety of educational initiatives, including a Steiner-modelled kindergarten.

	CONVENTIONAL VINES	BIODYNAMIC VINES
PRUNING:	End of October, when leaves have fallen.	When the moon is descending (late January or so), as days start getting longer.
WORKING THE LAND:	Nitrogen, potassium and phosphorus are used as artificial fertilisers.	A green manure of grasses and legumes encourages the development of a deep, structured soil with stable humus. Only light tools are used.
TREATMENTS:	Insecticides and anti-rotting chemicals are added.	Copper is added in small amounts. Vines growing in healthy soils are less prone to disease.
CLEARING BETWEEN VINES:	Toxic weed killer or heavy tractors are used that can damage soil.	Grasses are left to grow and cut if necessary. Sheep graze the vineyards.
BIODYNAMIC TREATMENTS:	None.	Biodynamic preparations (e.g. horn manure) are sprayed.

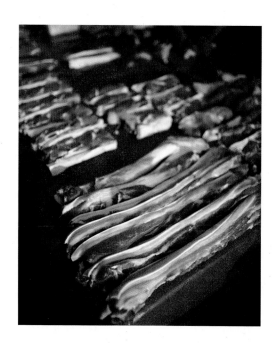

FROM TOP: Buying meat from the local farmer's market makes it easier to determine where the meat comes from and that the animals were raised with respect. The meat can be fresher and of superior quality too; freshly caught fish on display in a local market. OPPOSITE: A symbol of traditional Mexico, butterfly fishermen, named for the unique shape of their nets, used to fish in canoes, carved from a single tree-trunk in Lake Patzcuaro, but now, they have more modern, intensive measures for catching fish, and these unique nets are now used only as a tourist attraction.

ON THE SLOW PLATE Eating SLOW food is a varied and enjoyable experience, but some thought about the many types of food on offer is required in order to eat in this environmentally- and health-conscious manner. MEAT The consumption of animal products raises a number of ethical issues, the most obvious being those associated with eating animals in the first place. As long we are getting the essential nutrients from other sources, the human body does not need meat or fish to survive. However, many people choose animal produce for taste and gastronomic satisfaction, and these decisions should be respected as long as forethought is given to how the animal has lived its life, how it was killed and whether it is endangered.

Global meat consumption is believed to have escalated some 500 percent since 1950. This rising demand for animal feed has apparent environmental implications, with the potential disappearance of some species through overkill being paramount. Another is the growing demand for farmland to grow feed crops, a demand that is quickly destroying the rainforests and causing a host of environmental problems. With the high amount of energy required to produce meat (10 to 30 times more per kilogram than corn or soya), combined with the methane gas produced by cows (over 20 times more potent than carbon dioxide), farm animals are estimated to cause between 10 to 20 percent of the world's greenhouse gas emissions.

Eating veal pushes the ethical boundaries even further. While not inherently different from eating other young animals, it is the way much of veal is produced that is a cause for concern. In many cases, the calves are reared in crates,

packed into dark sheds and fed a poor, primarily liquid diet to ensure the prized white-coloured meat. As they suffer great distress and are more prone to disease, they normally are pumped full of antibiotics. While many countries have banned veal crates, they are still used in some areas, and the only way of stopping this torture is by saying no to veal.

Intensively farmed pigs can suffer hugely too, as the techniques used to rear these highly intelligent animals have become increasingly industrial in recent years. Sows have been transformed into meat-making machines. Not so long ago, five piglets a year was the norm for a sow, but with today's intensive breeding practices, 25 is not uncommon.

Those that are very serious about reducing their environmental footprint should consume fewer animal products, especially focusing on cutting out those from intensive, industrial farms. If buying meat or poultry, make sure they are from free-range farms that respect organic principles, animal welfare, conservation and preservation. While these farms are still rare in some parts of the world,

they are on the rise, thanks to increased consumer demand, which has made sourcing more sustainable and ethical choices easier. FISH According to the UN, one-quarter of the world's fisheries are either over-exploited or depleted, while another half is being fished to their maximum safe levels. The best cited example is cod and blue fin tuna (used to make sushi), both of which, in recent years, have gone from being plentiful to close to extinction. There are many other threatened species as global fish consumption has increased dramatically during the last century, endangering many fish populations.

The risks of over-fishing cannot be overstated, not only because the practice is leaving fewer fish in the sea, but also because it disrupts the wider food chain. While fishing quotas are in place in many areas, experts believe this is not sufficient to curb the decline in overall numbers. If current trends continue, the result could be a complete rearrangement of the ocean's ecosystems.

The shark population, for instance, is vital to the functioning of the marine environment. As top predators, they maintain the health of fish populations by regulating numbers and reducing the spread of disease. However, even

though many species of shark are endangered, the demand for shark's fins as food continues, despite the efforts of animal conservation and welfare organisations to curb their inhumane slaughter. Besides the morally questionable method of obtaining the fins, the fact is that shark meat is not as healthy as most other varieties of fish. As the predators at the top of the food chain, they accumulate very high mercury loads through their diets, which are toxic to humans. Focusing more on this potential toxicity may reduce the demand for fins and help curb the illegal finning process.

Drift nets used to catch tuna, swordfish, herring and other species are a problem too, as they can be many miles long and drag bycatch into the net along with the target species. With the technique of "bottom trawling", which entails dragging a fine net over the seabed in search of prawns, scallops, plaice and clams, among others species, more bycatch than actual target fish can get caught in the net. With large fishing vessels and their massive nets, endangered species such as dolphins, sea turtles, whales, sharks and seals often become part of the catch, as they too get caught up in the net. This mass-fishing technique also damages the seabed.

ENDANGERED FISH AND OTHER FISH TO BE AVOIDED:
Atlantic salmon (wild-caught)
Chilean sea bass
Cod
Flounder
Hake
Ling
Monkfish
Orange roughy
Red snapper
Shark
Sole
Sturgeon
Tuna (blue fin and non-dolphin friendly)
Catfish
Swordfish, marlin and saltfish
American and Canadian lobster
Blue crab
Caviar
Oysters (unless sustainably farmed)
Tiger prawn (except organic)
Whale
Seafood kept alive inhumanely in tanks or cages

Most varieties of fish are delicious and extremely nutritious for the body, and unlike livestock, they do not require enormous areas of land for feed. However, the massive global increase in consumption has occurred to the detriment of the environment and through a rise in industrial fishing and intensive aquaculture (or fish farming), both of which have environmental and social implications.

It has been estimated that about one-third of the world's fish are reared in farms. The vast majority of the salmon, trout and cod that is available today is farmed. To the more environmentally conscious, the financial savings associated with buying farmed fish (which are significantly cheaper than the wild variety) are outweighed by the fact that the damage inflicted on the marine ecosystem can be exacerbated as a result of the huge quantities of fish required to create the fish

farm in the first place. Furthermore, many environmental groups argue that the farms intensify pollution by churning out mineral and antibiotic-rich faeces that leaches straight into the surrounding waters, creating algal blooms that suffocate sea-bed life.

MAKING SMARTER CHOICES At the end of the day, it is up to us, as consumers, to help preserve what is left of the global marine world by minimising the negative impact of what we buy. Implement your own sustainable shopping policies by abiding by the following principles:

- Avoid meat from endangered animals.
- Choose meat and chicken from free-range farms that respect organic principles, animal welfare, conservation and preservation.
- Do not accept animal cruelty.
- Look for labels bearing standards relating to the environment, food safety and animal welfare (e.g. UK British Farm Standard).

FROM TOP: Over-fishing with nets has endangered many populations of fish; a large-scale fishing operation of yellow fin tuna. OPPOSITE: Antioxidant-rich and heart-healthy red grapes are one of nature's top superfoods.

- Do not buy crated or boxed veal.
- Be comfortable with the origin of the produce you choose.
- Avoid birds' nest and sharks' fin products.
- Be particular about what fish you buy by avoiding threatened and unsustainable varieties (see box on page 77).
- Buy fish from sustainable sources, such as Marine Stewardship Council-certified fish or the equivalent.
- Avoid endangered, young, undersized fish.
- If possible, find out how the fish was caught. Avoid those caught using mass-catching systems such as netting and trawling.
- Choose organic meat, poultry and daily produce where possible.

SUPERFOODS In the quest for ageless vitality, sleek, shining hair and radiant skin, nature's very own superfoods are without doubt the best supplements. Superfood is the term used to describe fruits, vegetables, nuts, seeds, fish and wholegrains that are enzymatically alive—powerhouses of vitamins, minerals, antioxidants (such as vitamins A, C, E and the trace elements selenium and zinc) and phytonutrients (plant chemicals). While these foods are not new, what is new is the scientific evidence supporting their role in protecting the body against diseases such as cancer. They can help to mop up free radicals from pollution and the general atmosphere. Choose those grown locally and organically when possible:

- Blueberries: Bursting with vitamin C, carotenoids and anthocyanidins, blueberries are believed to help reduce the risk of cancer and lower cholesterol. They also help strengthen the skin's collagen.
- Cranberries: The antioxidants in these vibrant red berries act as detoxifiers by helping to flush the kidneys.
- Flaxseeds: Naturally rich in Omega-3, Omega-6 EFAs (essential fatty acids) and vitamin E, flaxseeds contain powerful antioxidants that help to maintain healthy skin and hair, while also protecting the body against the extremely damaging effects of free radicals.
- Goji berries: Also called wolfberries, goji berries contain an estimated 500 times more vitamin C than oranges (gram for gram) while also being rich in protein and essential trace elements. They are widely used in traditional Chinese medicine.
- Nuts: Dry roasted, unsalted or raw nuts (especially Brazil nuts, walnuts, almonds and pistachios) are rich in heart-healthy monounsaturated fats while also being high in fibre, protein and vitamin E.
- Leafy greens: Spinach and many other delicious greens such as bok choy and broccoli are excellent sources of antioxidant vitamins C and E, beta-carotene, iron, calcium and B vitamins.
- Oats: Oats are packed with antioxidants, fibre and vitamins.

- Peppers: Capsicums are an excellent source of vitamin C and carotenoids such as beta-carotene that effectively mop up free radicals from the sun and environment.
- Pineapples: Pineapples are packed with the protein-digesting enzyme bromelain, that helps cleanse the body. They are also rich in vitamin C and phytonutrients.
- Pomegranates: These polyphenol-rich fruits help strengthen the skin's collagen and scavenge free radicals.
- Red grapes: The red pigment indicates an abundance of antioxidant anthocyanidins. They are rich in ellagic acid, an antioxidant, and flavonols, which cleanse the arteries.
- Root ginger: Ginger is rich in magnesium and acts as a natural hormone balancer for women. Taken as a tea, it is excellent for digestion, while also easing stomach upset.
- Oily fish: Salmon, tuna and other cold-water fish such as mackerel and halibut are rich in Omega-3 fatty acids, protein, vitamins A and D and minerals such as selenium and zinc.
- Tomatoes: The epitome of a cancer-fighting food, tomatoes are packed with vitamins A, C and E and lycopene, the antioxidant phytochemical (responsible for their rich red colour) that protects against both cancer and heart disease.
- Wheatgerm: Just a sprinkle of wheatgerm (nature's richest source of vitamin E) in cereals, yoghurts or while cooking ensures daily needs are met.

Planning a picnic is a fun way of making sure leftovers do not go to waste.

OPPOSITE (FROM TOP): Tasty homemade dressings can spice up leftover greens for a quick, delicious salad; a freshly tossed salad, using locally grown lettuce; if you keep stir-fry sauces on hand, a colourful stir-fry like this dish of sustainably farmed, local black king fish made at Evason Phuket is easy to prepare at a moment's notice.

WASTE TO WEALTH IN THE KITCHEN

While you can struggle over which meats, produce and food brands are best, one easy way of making a difference is simply by purchasing less. Minimise food wastage, and you will avoid putting unnecessary stress on both the environment and your wallet.

The following are some tips for getting maximum use of the food in your kitchen:

• Ensure all leftover food is correctly stored (refrigerated or frozen) and safe to reuse, as fruits and cooked rice are prone to spoilage.

• When preparing fresh ingredients, keep them separate and mix them bit by bit to the recipe. In this way, waste is minimised and leftover ingredients can be kept in the fridge for use in other meals.

• Keep a range of tried-and-tested stir-fry sauces like Phad Thai, Phad Krapao, sweet chilli and oyster sauce in the dry storage cupboard. They combine perfectly with leftover vegetables, meat or seafood (cooked or raw), making delicious stir-fries in a matter of minutes.

- Focus on a key leftover ingredient, such as pasta, rice potatoes, meat, vegetables or fruit, to make a quick, tasty meal. See the following simple recipes for ideas:

PASTA For a deliciously quick pasta salad: When cooking pasta, keep it separate from the sauce so any leftovers can make a salad. Add one part vinegar (balsamic), three parts extra virgin olive oil and some crushed basil leaves. Other leftovers can also be added such as chopped onion, diced tomatoes and salad greens or lightly cooked vegetables. Season with some freshly ground pepper and serve.

RICE For an easy fried rice: Leftover steamed rice becomes a delectable family meal. Simply fry a little chopped onion and chopped garlic in a non-stick pan until glazed. Add rice and leftover vegetables and/or strips of cooked meat or chicken. Toss gently while heating to ensure the rice does not stick. Season with some fish sauce, soya sauce, freshly milled sea salt, black pepper, chilli and chopped parsley or coriander (optional). If adding an egg, it should be done at the same time as the onion.

POTATOES For decadent fried potatoes: Cooked potatoes become amazing fried potatoes simply by slicing them and frying them in a little oil or butter. While not the most nutritious of meals, it is an irresistible occasional treat. If you have them on hand, some chopped bacon, onion and freshly chopped parsley can be added for extra taste.

For a perfectly yummy potato salad: Chop cooked potatoes, mix with either mayo or crème fraîche, chopped parsley or coriander and a few capers. Chill for one hour and serve. A healthy version can be also made with low-fat Greek yoghurt, instead of using mayo or crème fraîche.

MEAT For a Thai-style meat salad: Slice the meat into strips (reheat if necessary), and add some sliced onion, cucumber, celery and tomato. Season with lime juice, fish sauce, chopped garlic and coriander. Serve cold.

For a tasty meat and vegetable stir-fry: Lightly fry chopped fresh or leftover vegetables in a wok or non-stick pan. Add sliced meat strips and toss. Add stir-fry seasoning sauce, combine well and serve immediately.

For an exotic shoarma-style meat sandwich: Slice the meat into strips and lightly fry with a shoarma spice mix (available in most gourmet shops). Wrap cooked meat in pita bread with some fresh iceberg lettuce and chopped tomatoes.

VEGETABLES For an elegant antipasti starter: Chargrill leftover vegetables on an open flame or barbeque. Marinate them in extra virgin olive oil, fresh basil or other Italian herbs and season with freshly milled pepper. Eat the warm veggies as soon as possible.

For a fresh salsa: Crush leftover baked tomatoes and simmer in a pot with some garlic, chilli, a little vinegar and fresh herbs. Chill once cooked, add a little olive oil and some diced pickles (optional) and serve.

FRUIT Ensure that your fruit looks and tastes as it should before reusing.

For a sweet and fresh fruit cocktail: Dice fruit and add some fresh mint leaves. Chill for one hour before serving.

For a nutritious smoothie or shake: Soft creamy fruits like banana, mango or berries can be blended together. For extra goodness, some fresh milk or yoghurt can be added.

For a tasty summer fruit crush: Blend chopped fruit with ice cubes. Add some honey and serve immediately.

For a refreshing granita: Blend or juice the fruit, add some honey and pour onto a large wide tray. Freeze for 30 minutes before scraping the slightly frozen mass with a fork. Repeat about three times at 15-minute intervals until there is a crushed ice consistency. Serve in a tall glass with various chopped fruit or a mint leaf as decoration.

SLOW STYLE: WHOLESOME BEAUTY

Fashion is not something that exists only in dresses. Fashion is in the sky, in the street; fashion has to do with ideas, the way we live, what is happening.

- Coco Chanel

Although standards of beauty vary, what remains consistent across borders and has always been true throughout the centuries is our collective pursuit of real, natural beauty. Beauty and style may seem trivial in light of the perilous state of our planet. However, the clothes we wear and the beauty products we use can affect the environment in a negative way, or we can choose to tread lightly on the earth, crafting an appearance that is beautiful on the surface but also one that leaves us feeling wholesome, one that reflects our personal beliefs and a commitment to protecting our planet.

Just imagine a daily skincare regime that uses the very best of nature's ingredients, grown in regions where organic agriculture is normal practice and where the wellbeing of the local community and the earth is paramount. With the continuing interest in natural and organic skincare, this is possible, and in the words of many beauty experts, is the only way to real ageless beauty—self-assured radiance in which character, humour and vibrancy are freely expressed and celebrated.

The way an individual approaches fashion can both minimise his or her carbon footprint while also becoming an outlet for promoting climate change in a public manner. The clothes you choose can, in effect, advertise personal ideals. What's more, the choices for the eco-friendly fashionista have never been more extensive. Not so long ago, the terms "ecologically sustainable" and "designer" seemed mutually exclusive. Anything labelled "eco-friendly" was handmade, plant-dyed and not in any way fashionable. Hardcore ecologists rejected the aesthetics and vibrancy of modern design. Times have changed; doing the right thing for our planet no longer means sacrificing looking good.

Consumers can wield a tremendous tool to prevent climate change: purchasing power. Fashion and beauty products illustrate this point explicitly, and as the market for natural and organic products expands, our small, day-to-day, seemingly insignificant choices will continue to shape this burgeoning industry—for either the better or the worse.

Placing freshly ground spices and herbs—which smell delicious and are good for the skin—in a compress is a great way to use natural ingredients during a massage.
OPPOSITE: Nature has always been at the root of fashion, as shown by the the bright red resin of the dragons' blood tree in Yemen, which has been used for centuries to make cosmetics.
PREVIOUS: By using natural products and limiting water usage, luxurious beauty rituals such as bubble baths can be enjoyed in a way that minimises environmental impact.

Woman applying a facemask prepared from fresh natural ingredients. OPPOSITE (FROM TOP): Six Senses Spas use a variety of pure, freshly prepared natural ingredients during many of their signature treatments; amenities found in the Six Senses guestrooms are wrapped in recyclable, natural packaging.

SKINCARE Achieving and maintaining a glowing complexion naturally, while holding back the hands of time, is certainly possible, as long as skin is adequately nourished from within. In addition to a fresh, seasonal diet brimming with the skin's superfood essentials (see page 79), a natural skincare regime that works in harmony with the body to enhance cellular regeneration is the ideal prescription (both in terms of the health of the individual and of the environment) for beautiful, radiant skin at any age.

While anti-ageing skincare and sustainability are not obvious partners, an increasing number of skincare companies are producing products packed with deliciously natural ingredients, created with an innate passion and craftsmanship and a genuine commitment for protecting our planet.

The skin has different needs at different stages of life, and the market for results-driven, anti-ageing skincare is bigger than ever. Traditionally the market has been dominated by products in which the inclusion of every ingredient is scrupulously calculated to deliver precise amounts of wrinkle-defying benefits. But now that it is medically accepted that the body absorbs significant amounts of what is used on the skin, consumers are becoming more cautious about what they are buying—hence, the advent of an advanced skincare category that meticulously blends natural ingredients and is supported by extensive scientific research, bridging the gap between science and nature. While some of these products do not claim to be organic, they are free from suspect chemicals like parabens (the preservatives that help prevent microbial contamination), petrochemicals, artificial colours and other synthetic chemicals. What's more, with the continuing refinement in the extraction of active properties from natural ingredients, the results and benefits of this super natural skincare may soon match the performance of synthetic counterparts.

While all products need preservatives to maintain their shelf life, safety and efficacy, this is even more important with natural and organic products that are more prone to oxidation and damage from harmful bacteria and fungi. However, vitamin E and certain plant oils, rather than harsh, synthetic chemicals, are widely used to preserve and safeguard these natural products.

As we strive to clean up our world, packaging is as important as the actual ingredients in a product. For most consumers, convenience is a priority, but all too often the excessive glossy packaging ends up in an already overflowing landfill. Plastic is traditionally the easiest and most cost effective packaging option for beauty products, but with the advances in sustainable packaging

technology (such as the use of zero-waste, 100 percent post-consumer newsprint and plant-based packaging that is fully compostable), there is no excuse for manufacturers not to use recyclable and biodegradable options when packaging their goods. By ensuring that an absolute barrier is generated through effective airtight packaging, the safety and shelf life of natural products can be extended.

NATURAL VERSUS ORGANIC CERTIFICATION

When it comes to classifying cosmetics, there are no hard and fast rules. The "natural" and "organic" labels appear on numerous products, and consumers often become genuinely confused when trying to differentiate between them.

Natural or organic skincare does not necessarily mean chemical free. Every ingredient is a chemical, regardless of its origin. Water, for example, is a chemical and is not

ANIMAL CRUELTY

Many countries have banned animal testing for cosmetics, but this has not stopped products that have been tested on animals from appearing on the market. According to animal rights campaigners, millions of animals are subjected to tests every year for products ranging from hair dyes to moisturisers and deodorants. The most notorious of tests, which continues to be performed, is the LD50 or Lethal Dose 50 test, during which animals are gradually given increasing doses of the test substance until half of them have died. In eye irritation studies, chemicals are slowly added to the animals' (normally rabbits) eyes until irritation (often severe) occurs. Until there is a worldwide ban on animal testing, it is up to us, the consumer, to decide if intense animal suffering is a reasonable price to pay for vanity.

certifiable. As many skincare products contain water, none of these can be labelled as 100 percent organic or natural.

Natural cosmetics market themselves as containing primarily plant or mineral ingredients. The organic label tells how an ingredient has been grown. It does not explain how beneficial the ingredient or product is to the body. While scientific research has yet to definitively prove that plant-based cosmetics are healthier and more effective in turning back the hands of time, those who use them often appreciate just how good they feel on the skin and swear by their effectiveness in maintaining a radiant, youthful glow.

Many countries have their own certification bodies to ensure that the products produced in that country (both natural and organic) meet certain standards. Once these standards are met, approval seals can then placed on the label. However, certification costs money and prohibits some, generally smaller, companies (whose products may be completely natural or organic) from having a seal on their products.

A product can still be considered natural even if it contains some synthetic ingredients. The United States Department of Agriculture (USDA), for example, permits the placement of its seal on products that are 95 percent or more organic, with the remaining 5 percent of ingredients having to come from approved natural sources (www.usda.com). Similarly, the standards of the French certification body ECOCERT state that at least 95 percent of ingredients must be of natural origin (www.ecocert.org). On the other hand, the British Soil Association allows a product to be certified if it contains up to 5 percent non-organic ingredients, but only if there are no organic alternatives (www.soilassociation.org). A number of certifiers exist in Australia, each with their own specific certification criteria, such as Australian Certified Organic (ACO) and Nasaa (www.australianorganic.com.au, www.nasaa.com.au). However, in some countries, a product need only have a shred of organic content to earn a seal of approval.

When purchasing skin and body products, always check the labels. If a product claims to be natural, read what it contains, and most importantly, note what is left out (e.g. synthetic preservatives, fragrances, petrochemicals and other suspect chemical derivatives). Look for certification (natural or organic) from a credible certifying body, bearing in mind that while most ethical products bear the seal, there are equally genuine manufacturers sharing this commitment that cannot afford to be certified. Also, check where the ingredients are produced and if the packaging is biodegradable or recyclable. In this way, you can ensure that the products you choose are gentle, nourishing and kind to the environment.

FASHION In the fashion world, seasons dictate style. They provide a safe and clear-cut guide to wardrobe essentials, and expectations grow around each new season's colours, fabrics and unique looks. However, with the world's increasingly erratic and unpredictable weather patterns, retailers and designers are resorting to climate experts for advice on the most appropriate clothes for the changeable seasons. With the shift in nature's patterns comes a new message—one that is less about dressing for the seasons and more about wearing what works for you and your environment. Being green and smart matches a growing trend of consumers choosing understated luxury, as ostentatious labels are being replaced by alluring items made with finely crafted natural materials.

LUXURY HORIZONS
BY DR JEM BENDELL

After 10 years as an author, educator, consultant on sustainable business and an advisor to the UN, Dr Jem Bendell turned his attention to the luxury industry. With Anthony Kleanthous, Bendell wrote the 2007 report for WWF, "Deeper Luxury: Quality and Style When the World Matters", helping to put the environment on the industry's agenda. He explains his philosophy as follows:

"I saw the potential for luxury products and services to prefigure the way we will consume in a just and sustainable society. Not the shallow 'luxury' of conspicuous brands, but the deeper luxury inherent in the treasuring of the materials, people, traditions and crafts that bring products and experiences into being.

As the financial crisis unfolded, many newspapers and politicians told us not to panic and carry on shopping to help fuel the economy and stave off economic disaster. Initially, governments propped up companies to continue producing the things we were not buying. How did we reach a point where the quantity of shopping mattered more than its quality? But the collapse of confidence in an ever-increasing consumer society is inspiring a deep shift in values, a shift that may ultimately result in a change for the better.

Firstly, I predict a broad change in the way people view wealth and success, in that consumption will no longer be seen as an end in itself. By questioning consumption, we are starting to connect with the environmental awareness that research has found is growing worldwide. As associations are made between how we consume and how this consumption affects the environment, the implications for fashion, and business in general, are huge.

The second change will involve people turning away from the simplistic view of the West always being best. The economic crisis is creating a reordering of world power that is being reflected in a shifting political and cultural influence. Consequently, people are starting to look to a wider range of traditions for ideas and esteem. This does not mean turning away from seeking a better life and society, but rediscovering past traditions for a new and better life.

These changes will be embodied through fashion too. The paradox is that while we consider luxury to be highly personal, it is highly socialised at the same time. Consequently, as society changes, so will our concept of luxury and what we consider to be a luxury brand.

Authentic and desired luxury brands of the future will rightly reflect the wisdom and creativity of the diverse cultures of the world. Ultimately, this new notion of 'luxury' will become the norm, a luxury that in its design will help both those involved in its creation and the planet itself. The entrepreneurs, executives and experts behind the Authentic Luxury Network are committed to this new, better and even more luxurious model."
- Dr Jem Bendell (www.authenticluxury.net)

Model wearing alluring eco-couture cocktail dress made from recycled Indian saris by Nathan Jenden, featured on the EcoChic Shanghai runway.

OPPOSITE: Chic, sexy and sustainable creations by designer Linda Loudermilk.

According to the 2007 WWF report "Deeper Luxury: Quality and Style When the World Matters" by Dr Jem Bendell and Anthony Kleanthous (www.wwf.org.uk/deeper luxury/report.html), the luxury industry is evolving radically, with the latest definition of luxury having as much to do with sustainability as with quality. Further, the report highlights that luxury brands are capable of making a greater positive impact on people and our planet than any other product or service.

After all, money talks, and the large investments people make in luxury brands—the price tag of some designer goods can often equal the annual income of a small village in India—can affect what goods are produced and how they are made. The chain of production of even a simple dress is long; before fabric reaches the factories, the raw material needs to be grown, killed or manufactured. Hence, if improvements are made throughout this industry, the effects would be widespread. Additionally, the practices of luxury brands could also have a ripple effect, as more affordable brands mimic the trends set by luxury names. What's more, it is no secret that labour standards in many areas of the fashion industry leave a lot to be desired, so conscientious consumers can help both the environment and people's quality of life in many areas around the world.

As our social dynamic is changing, savvy consumers are rejecting profit-driven brands lacking in substance and are recognising a top-quality product as one that generates the greatest benefit to all involved in its production. By supporting ethical designers with minimal carbon footprints, we can actually do our part to save our planet—one purchase at a time.

DESIGN WITH A HIGHER PURPOSE:
LINDA LOUDERMILK

Before it was cool to be green, Linda Loudermilk saw the light. Dubbed the "Vivienne Westwood of eco" by *Elle* magazine, this couture and eco-designer has linked luxury and eco principles in an unprecedented way. Through her designs (e.g. sculptured shift dresses and jeans with alluring cuts), she has made sustainability sexy.

Loudermilk began producing her eco-friendly designs by sourcing sustainable fabrics made from pesticide- and toxin-free materials. Forming relationships with manufacturers that share her ideals, she works with companies that strive to avoid pollution and have a general consciousness about their effect on the planet.

By weaving lace and pieces of rich fabric into clothes made from natural fabrics, she found a way to celebrate the beauty of the earth through fashion. Working with *sasawashi* (a Japanese allergen-free leaf), bamboo, sea cell, soya and reclaimed lace, among other textiles, her clothing brings conscientiousness to the catwalk.

She trademarked the term luxury eco™, becoming the first designer to combine luxury and eco qualities so definitively. By establishing the luxury eco™ "Stamp of Approval", she also seeks to honour other companies that share her mission. The stamp implies that the products or services labelled as such are not only eco-friendly, but also superior in quality. Loudermilk explains the rationale behind her designs as follows:

"Eco is about our core, not our shell. By choosing what we buy based on utmost respect for ourselves and all living objects here on earth, this reaches our core. When I made it to the Paris runways and the dizzy heights of fashion, I should have been rejoicing in the accolades. Instead, I felt empty. I was creating beauty, but beauty without soul. I then realised I wanted to make a difference, to change the way people think about the earth. This difference is luxury eco™—a journey to self-knowledge that leads to self-respect. When we really know who we are, then we can dress

accordingly. However, we tend to know more about what's best for our closest friends rather than ourselves.

Raw self-expression is the future of fashion. Call it, 'Punk, I want to be myself style'. These old-world preservationists that disrespect our planet are no longer cool or sexy. But luxury eco™ is. It's new, it's fresh and it's raw. Wabi-sabi is the new chic. Like understanding the beauty of a crack in the pavement by planting it with dandelions or a rip in your skirt—ask your tailor to add a chiffon godet. Take the ebb and flow of life and make it your unique product. Spend money on what is valuable. Pass up all the costume jewellery at the department store and invest in a gold watch. The rest is cluttering your vision of how rich your soul really is.

I created luxury eco™ and the Luxury Stamp of Approval to help people navigate the sea of faux design, almost-there quality and supposed 'natural' (yet drenched in pesticides). We are drowning in too many inferior and dangerous products. By purchasing many of these, we are suppressing our ability to recognise quality and craftsmanship and settling for less. Our body has adapted to feeling less healthy, and we don't really know it.

When you wear one of my eco-chic garments you not only feel sexy and stylish, you feel clean, clear and ultimately incredibly proud of your choice. Now you have something unique to talk about. It's made of *sasawashi*! Just feel it. It goes deep. Choose with a fierce heart."

- Linda Loudermilk

Silk—as in this sustainably produced organic silk top— is a fabric that can easily be made according to organic and ethical guidelines.
OPPOSITE: Sustainable ready-to-wear bamboo jersey backless dress by Lara Miller.

SUSTAINABLE FABRICS The market for sustainable fabrics such as organic cotton, linen, silk, hemp and bamboo is growing, thanks to a new wave of consumers and more eco-conscious designers and retailers. Formerly the realm of the flower power brigade, today, these materials are the foundations of many of the exquisitely designed clothes being worn by top celebrities and models.

Like food, organic fibres can be grown and manufactured free from pesticides and other chemical additives. When it comes to materials certified as organic, committed companies will stand out because guidelines on sustainable fabric production are widely available, and garments that comply will be clearly labelled. However, it is still up to the consumer to ask the right questions regarding sustainability, fair trade and ethics, so they are more informed about what they are buying.

The most commonly used sustainable fibres include the following:

• Cotton: Conventional cotton is the most widely used natural-fibre cloth in clothing. It is a soft fibre that grows around the seeds of the cotton plant, native to the Americas, India and Africa. The fibre is spun into yarn or thread that is used to make cotton. It is no secret, however, that a huge range of synthetic substances are used in the manufacture of conventional cotton, from chlorine bleaches to heavy metal dyes and harsh chemical treatments that minimise shrinking. On the other hand, organic cotton is free from pesticides, herbicides, or insecticides, and only natural dyes are used during manufacture. A new type of "naturally-coloured cotton" that grows in shades of green and brown and is completely free from synthetic dyes is now coming onto the market. It has the added benefit of retaining the vibrancy of its colour even after extensive washing.

- Jute: Extracted from the stem and outer skin of the plants *Corchorus capsularis* and *Corchorus olitorius*, jute is one of nature's strongest vegetable fibres and ranks second only to cotton in terms of production quantity and range of uses. The plant thrives in hot, humid climates and is grown primarily in India, with smaller quantities grown in Myanmar and Nepal. It is used to make floor coverings, non-wovens, paper pulp, textiles, handicrafts and fashion accessories. As a biodegradable and sustainable textile, jute is increasingly being used by designers. However, further innovation is required in production and processing technologies to reduce the cost of manufacture, in order to make it a more profitable option.

- Silk: The silk that is most commonly used in clothing is obtained from cocoons made by the larvae of the mulberry silkworm (*Bombyx mori*). The process of cultivating and harvesting silkworm threads is a big business throughout Asia, especially in India and China. Silk can easily be created according to approved organic and ethical guidelines. In fact, the silk produced by local weavers in small remote villages is already being produced in an organic environment and is the purest. Silk fabric, when produced by weavers on handlooms, has a near zero-energy footprint and satisfies most of the guidelines for sustainable silk production. It is the silk produced in large power-loomed textile factories that can prove suspect in terms of its sustainability credentials. When choosing sustainable and eco-friendly silk,

look for silks dyed using low-impact and fibre reactive or vegetable dyes. The silk fabric should not be weighted or have any easy-care or protective finishes. Also, as with all fabrics, check if the silk garments were produced according to fair trade principles.

- Hemp: The history of the *Cannabis sativa* plant is more closely associated with drugs than clothing, rope or paper. Banned for years in many countries, it is back, due to its sustainable credentials. The hemp plant is easy, quick, inexpensive and safe to grow. Its ecological footprint is considerably smaller than that of most other plants used in clothing. As the plants grow very quickly and densely, it is difficult for weeds to take hold, thereby naturally eliminating the need for herbicides and artificial fertilisers. It requires little irrigation, and the long, durable fibres make it suitable for spinning with limited processing. Almost half of the world's industrial hemp supply is grown in China, with most of the remainder being cultivated in Chile, France, the Democratic People's Republic of Korea and Spain. One of its key environmental attributes is the ability of the whole plant to be utilised productively: the seed (which is really like a type of nut) can be pressed to make hemp seed oil, which has a range of uses, from lubricants, ink and cosmetics to the manufacture of plastics for furniture and CD cases; the multifunctional pithy core can be made into animal bedding and a type of concrete used to build walls; and the fibres are widely used in the manufacture of carpets and upholstery, while also proving to be a sustainable replacement to fibreglass in skateboards and surfboards. In China, scientists are using de-

gumming technologies to "cottonise" hard hemp fibres into fine, softer and more workable textile fibres.

- Bamboo: One of the sturdiest and most rapidly growing plants on earth, bamboo, like hemp, grows quickly with little maintenance. It is biodegradable too and quickly regenerates without replanting. It can be made into an attractive, soft and highly durable fabric with a natural sheen that closely resembles silk or cashmere. In addition to textiles, versatile bamboo is used to make paper, furniture, pens, sandals, lamps, chopsticks, baskets, tiles, diesel fuels and musical instruments, among other things.

- Coconut: Demand for fabrics made from coconut husks and shells is growing as the strength, durability and anti-bacterial properties of this sustainable fibre, known as coir, makes it an attractive option for

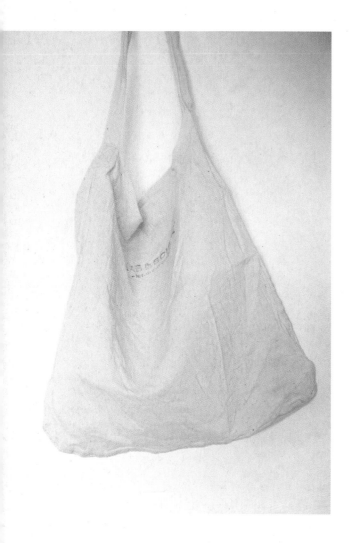

Limit the number of plastic bags that you throw away by using an organic cotton bag to carry home the goods you purchase. OPPOSITE: At Six Senses resorts and spas, sustainably produced linen, cotton, and other eco-friendly fabrics are used for the uniforms of staff, to outfit the rooms and are available for sale at Six Senses Gallerys.

manufacturers and designers. Coir fibre is extracted from the husk of the coconut. It has one of the highest concentrations of the natural polymer lignin, which gives it incredible strength. It is used mainly in furniture padding, matting, ropes, twines and as filling for mattresses. In addition, its resilience and biodegradability are well suited for use in geotextiles, insulation material and in boats. Coconuts are typically grown by a large number of small-scale farmers, most notably in India, Sri Lanka, the Philippines and Indonesia, who take husks to local mills for fibre extraction. The fibre is extracted by hand from either green coconut husks or mature brown ones. As a renewable natural material, coir has enormous potential for uptake in many profitable applications (see the following website for more information: www.natural fibres2009.org/en/fibres/index.html).

SHOPPING WITH A CONSCIENCE

While the real changes the world needs are not for sale in even the greenest shop, shopping can make a big difference to the world. Environmentally conscious fashion choices mean reducing not only post-consumer refuse, but also pre-consumer waste, pollution and human and animal suffering.

As more and more designers and manufacturers create an array of appealing products with environmental and ethical concerns in mind, finding satisfying answers to consumers' growing list of concerns is becoming easier. Through careful and smart wardrobe management, it is possible to support healthy, clean industry and look and feel great at the same time. Just keep the following guidelines in mind:

- Shop smart: Why buy questionable products when safer alternatives are widely available? Look beyond vague claims on packages to find hard facts.
- Buy green: While there are an increasing number of eco-friendly items for sale, remember the greenest garments are those you already own. No further resources are required to get them to you.
- Buy local: Where possible, buy locally manufactured clothing from local outlets.
- Buy organic: Always read the label and choose naturally-dyed, organic fibres.
- Less is more: Buy less clothing overall. When you do buy, choose versatile classic styles and colours that will not age.
- Buy vintage or used: Give cast-offs a second life by buying from vintage shops and websites specialising in vintage clothing. You will most probably be supporting charitable work in the process.
- Keep clothes longer: Whatever you buy, take good care of it. Learn how to sew, or find a local tailor or seamstress.
- Wash well: Experts attest that the greatest environmental burden from clothes is not in their construction and distribution, but in their cleaning. Washing clothes involves large quantities of water, energy and chemicals. Greener threads can normally be cold washed and line dried. Turn articles inside out and wash them at the lowest temperature possible (see pages 120–121).
- Do not throw it away: Do not let changing trends dictate. If clothes are in good condition, donate them to a charity or to the increasing number of eco-designers who specialise in salvaging fabrics for reuse in completely new styles.

SLOW PARENTING

learning for the future

SLOW PARENTING: LEARNING FOR THE FUTURE
The wild world is becoming so remote to children that they miss out.
An interest in the natural world doesn't grow as it should. Nobody is
going to protect the natural world unless they understand it.

- Sir David Attenborough, *BBC Wildlife* magazine, 2008

No one knows what kind of world we will inhabit in 10 years, not to mention in 40 years, when the
children born now will be decision makers. How do we know what to teach them? However, one
thing is clear: if we don't instil in them a love of nature and a genuine desire to protect it, it is unlikely
that the world's beauty will survive intact, to be enjoyed by future generations.

Few can deny that having and bringing up children is a uniquely rewarding experience. However,
as most parents will also attest, it can be intensely challenging too. Parents have an inherent concern
for the welfare of their children, including a desire to feed them well and to look after their health. In
our increasingly toxic world, more and more parents are looking for natural solutions to various
childhood issues, from dietary problems and behavioural issues to emotional difficulties—all of which
can prevent children from achieving their full potential.

It is well recognised in the Western world that over the last few decades there has been a steady
decline in the percentage of meals that children eat in the home. Not surprisingly, sharing family
meals has been associated with better nutrition in children, as it encourages them to eat a wider
variety of foods, while at the same time showing them that family meals can be fun.

By helping children to taste, smell and recognise even the simplest of fresh, local foods and
offering them a knowledge of where food comes from, they too will start to appreciate the real
pleasures of family mealtimes. Not only can interaction with food help improve their nutrition for life, it
can also stimulate an interest and appreciation for the natural world as a whole—the very animals
and plants we depend on for sustenance.

Children begin their life journey with the smallest of ecological footprints. By helping them to live
clean, creative, productive and sustainable lives, we can keep it this way over the long term, helping
children to grow up to become fair custodians of our earth.

Child holding a bowl of
freshly gathered herbs from
the garden.
OPPOSITE: A young girl learns
how to make a craft from
an array of recycled
materials at Just Kids!,
Evason Phuket, Thailand.
PREVIOUS: Silhouettes of
children at dusk, enjoying
the great outdoors.

Children earnestly learning their lessons at the Green School in Bali, Indonesia. OPPOSITE (FROM TOP): Mother and daughter exploring the natural wonders of Soneva Fushi, Maldives, by bike; whimsical papier-mâché blowfish created with recycled newspapers by children at Just Kids!, Evason Phuket, Thailand.

HEALTH AND THE ENVIRONMENT

Childhood disease continues to be a serious burden on families and society as rates of asthma, certain cancers, birth defects and other developmental disabilities, such as attention deficit hyperactivity disorder (ADHD) and autism, continue to increase. These disabilities prevent children from reaching their full potential. The Centers for Disease Control and Prevention has estimated that 17 percent of children under 18 in the US has one or more developmental disabilities, and the consensus is that these problems are on track to increase even further in the future (for more information, see www.cdc.gov).

While there are multiple risk factors at play with all of these conditions, much research points to the role of the environment as a significant contributor. Air pollutants such as particulate matter, ground level ozone, pesticides as well as chemicals in drinking water, food and toys have been implicated. Research has shown that pervasive toxic substances such as mercury, lead, polychlorinated biphenyls (PCBs), dioxins and pesticides can contribute to neuro-behavioural and cognitive disorders. Human exposure to these substances is rampant, and as knowledge about their toxicity increases, the "safe" threshold of exposure is being revised downward. Limiting exposure to toxins can prevent childhood disorders, and while many governments around the world are trying to clean up their environments, others do not realise the urgency. It is every parent's responsibility to ensure that they are doing their bit by confronting these issues and making cleaner choices for their own health and that of future generations.

WHOLESOME CHOICES FOR CHILDREN Children are vulnerable, and their development is a delicate biological process guided by their body's hormones, acting at exquisitely low levels to affect every cell, organ and bodily function. Exposure to any toxic chemical during these critical stages of development can disrupt this subtle process, resulting in lifelong health implications.

An estimated 1,500 to 2,000 new chemicals are brought onto the market every year, with many of these are not even listed as active ingredients in products. Some plastic teething toys, for example, have been renamed "toxic lollipops". While governments around the world have banned and recalled thousands of toys due to their high levels of toxins, many still remain on the market.

Safer alternatives are available. The following guidelines can help you make the best choices for your child:

- Buy PVC-free: PVC releases toxins into the environment through every part of its life cycle, from manufacturing to disposal.

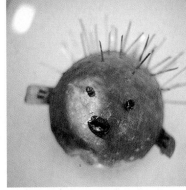

- Choose wood: Look for Forest Stewardship Council (FSC)-certified wooden toys. Wooden toys can last for generations. Untreated and unpainted wood is the safest choice for kids of all ages.
- Recycle toys: When your child is done with a toy, wooden and other long-lasting toys can be passed on to a relative, friend or given a new life through a second-hand outlet.
- Power down: Batteries have become ubiquitous in most toys today. When buying for younger children in particular, decide if the battery-powered toy is worth the waste (and the noise). If batteries are required, choose rechargeable alternatives.
- Buy organic: Choose stuffed toys made from organic and naturally-dyed textiles like cotton, bamboo, hemp and wool.
- Non-toxic paints: Select toys painted with water-based and low-volatile organic compound (VOC) or no-VOC paint.
- Running wild: Let children enjoy the great outdoors. It is easy and free.

GREENING THE FAMILY Going green should be a family affair, so make it fun. Pop some popcorn, gather recycled notepads and let the family green machine take flight.

A discussion that emphasises the importance of conservation can have a huge impact. For instance, children will not turn off lights if they do not think that it is important to do so. For a more efficient, less resource-hungry home, each family member must contribute and jointly implement new, more environmentally friendly practices.

Begin by prioritising some broad areas of discussion such as energy use, water use, laundry, gardening, heating, the kitchen and

FROM TOP: A child's drawing of a rising ocean flooding Sydney's Opera House and other iconic landmarks; young girl placing plastic bottles in a recycling bin.
OPPOSITE (FROM TOP): Papier-mâché fish, pig and snake by kids at Just Kids!, Evason Phuket, Thailand; tissue box made from recycled materials.

family meals. Brainstorm and agree on one action item per topic. Create a sense of ownership by assigning family members to each task, and make your goals more manageable by discussing how they can be achieved and setting a time frame. Also, keeping everyone on track can be easier when you post goals through the house before scheduling the next meeting. You will often find that children will enjoy the responsibility and ownership given to them. They may even become tougher taskmasters than their parents. As the home becomes greener and children more inventive, further topics can be added to the list and responsibilities extended.

YOUR OWN EARTH HOUR One easy way of making a difference and emphasising the importance of the environment to your children is by starting your own Earth Hour at home. Earth Hour was started in Sydney in 2007 by the World Wildlife Fund, when more than two million homes and businesses switched off their lights for one hour. In 2008, the message had grown into a global sustainability movement, with 50 million people switching off their lights. Earth Hour 2009 had a goal of one billion people switching off their lights as part of a global vote. This global call to action for every individual, business and community to stand up and take control over the future of their planet reveals how the importance of environmental conservation is growing around the world.

However, rather than just joining Earth Hour once a year, do it once a month or even more frequently at home. Switch off all lights, TVs, computers, stereos and other appliances, and switch on family time. Light candles, enjoy a wholesome family meal together, play games or sit and chat. Young children will get

especially excited about it and may enlist their friends and other families in the effort (see www.earthhour.org for more information).

TVS AND COMPUTERS Children need time to reflect and let their imaginations flow. TVs, DVDs and computers are an inevitable part of growing up, for families that can afford them. While you should limit their use, you can also capitalise on their inevitable presence by ensuring your children are watching more about the natural world around them. It may surprise you how much they enjoy it and how much it can influence their adult life.

ENCOURAGING CREATIVITY

Children start learning from the moment they are born. By trial and error, they learn to sit up, walk, run and jump. By experience, they learn what their five senses are. By watching others doing daily tasks, their physical dexterity improves. They see natural events like running water and the sun shining, and they make deductions about how the world works. Children want to learn, and they will absorb important lessons almost entirely voluntarily.

Once formal education begins, this natural curiosity ceases to be voluntary, as learning is determined by the demands of the curriculum. Primary education sows the seeds of lifelong learning. However, it has been said that our current education system, which demands that children memorise, repeat what is shown and conform, is geared to produce clones—not creative and curious human beings.

In *Out of Our Minds: Learning to Be Creative*, Sir Ken Robinson says that schools are failing to equip children with the qualities they need to become empowered human beings able to address boldly the legacy of problems

(environmental, social and economic) that they will face as adults. Robinson says, "There is another crisis today in addition to the climate crisis. It's the crisis of human resources and in particular a failure to tap the full potential of human creativity and imagination." Although young people naturally have these qualities in abundance, by the time they emerge from formal education many do not. "If the goal of an education system is to create citizens who aspire to be creative, intelligent guardians of the earth, a more diverse child-centred education with subjects that nurture creative thinking is needed," says Robinson. He calls for a new paradigm based on a more organic metaphor: "Gardeners and farmers know they cannot make plants grow: plants grow themselves. Gardeners and farmers provide the conditions in which they will do that best. That's the challenge for education—to provide the best conditions in which the individual talents of all students will flourish."

I believe our only hope for the future is to adopt a new conception of human ecology, one in which we start to reconstitute our conception of the richness of human capacity. Our education system has mined our minds in the way that we strip-mine the earth: for a particular commodity. And for the future, it won't serve us. We have to rethink the fundamental principles on which we're educating our children. And the only way we'll do it is by seeing our creative capacities for the richness they are, and seeing our children for the hope they are.

- Sir Ken Robinson (www.sirkenrobinson.com)

A SCHOOL FOR THE 21ST CENTURY

A vision of shaping the minds of the next generation in order to help them become ecologically responsible citizens led Bali-based John Hardy and his wife Cynthia to create the Green School (see www.greenschool.org). The Green School is designed to be a fertile environment for future thinkers and creative problem solvers, knowledgeable about all aspects of life and capable of being leaders in a changing and challenging world. While the traditional subjects such as mathematics, languages, arts and science are at the core of the curriculum, each student's creative potential is also continually challenged while he or she is actively learning how to offset carbon emissions, start businesses, design and build lasting sustainable buildings and farm organically by helping to grow the very food that is eaten by the students in school.

Set on 8 hectares (20 acres) of land on Bali's Ayung River, just 15 minutes from Ubud in central Bali, the school lives in perfect symbiosis with the natural ecology. It is constructed almost entirely of packed earth and bamboo. The 75 small campus buildings are cooled and powered by micro hydropower, solar power and bio-diesel; the organic gardens provide fruit, vegetables, herbs and even cocoa for the school's kitchen. The school's five water buffalo feed a biogas system that extracts methane, and the leftover waste gets fed to worms, creating a rich compost that goes straight back into the school's gardens.

The unique curriculum aims to instil in the children social responsibility, honesty, ethics and compassion by focusing on providing a well-rounded, holistic education.

Moreover, on a separate campus across the river in Sibang, Abiansemal, Green Camp is an activity-based, extra-curricular centre with residential and day camps for students aged from seven to 18. This "learning by doing" environment focuses on the study of permaculture and sustainability, while also offering a variety of activities that encourage entrepreneurialism and creativity.

Global studies, life-skills training, team outward-bound activities and the development of creative self-expression are core elements of all camps. Green Camp students sleep in cosy, custom-built yurts (a tent-like structure) and share access to all the Green School's amenities across the river.

John Hardy explains the unique and compelling philosophy of the Green School and Green Camp, saying: "We are nurturing current and future generations of children to interface directly with their living environment and to engage with society in new ways, so that the changes we collectively make to address the environmental imperative will have longevity. We believe that Green School's diverse creative education can achieve this. We are committed to delivering generations of global citizens who are knowledgeable about and inspired to take responsibility for the sustainability of the world."

STIMULATING THE SENSES The five senses have an inescapable influence on the development of creativity, emotions and the nervous system in children. These perceptions are present from the very earliest stages of development. Every day, through the precise workings of the body, growing children receive a non-stop barrage of sensations from the environment and culture in which they live. Research has shown that the greater the abundance of stimuli that children are exposed to, the better the possibility of developing an intelligent and balanced personality, well suited to deal with the complex web of life.

Our progressive separation from the rhythms of the natural world—its climate, vegetation, colours, smells and tastes—in contrast to an increasingly anonymous and standardised urban environment, can be detrimental to future generations. For instance, some anthropologists say that pollution in bigger cities can induce a conditioned reflex that causes a kind of apnoea (temporary cessation of breathing) that can lead to progressive weakening of the sense of smell.

The same can be said for food. The repetitive taste of many fast foods, caused by the use of artificial flavourings, is generating a progressive decrease in taste sensitivity. The result is that we fail to appreciate the varied and ever-changing flavours of natural foods such as local fruits and vegetables.

CHILDREN AND FOOD It is time to rediscover nature by introducing it to children through food. Connecting young people with food is integral to both their future and that of the food industry. Local foods are especially important in this cognitive journey, as they reflect the culture that produced them and represent a healthy relationship to the world. A child is never too young to start learning about the significance of food. Letting babies play with food (while supervised) helps them understand the feel, taste and smell of foods. By the age of five or six, children should be able to distinguish the four basic tastes (sweet, salty, bitter and sour).

Make meals fun by asking children to describe the differences in the taste of foods they are eating. Does the food taste good or bad, sweet or salty? Those that are especially interested can write or draw their perceptions. By the age of 12, when their analytical capacities are more advanced, children manage to critically examine sensory perceptions, and they can start cooking meals on their own. By actively engaging children during meals, of all ages, they will learn to enjoy the wholesome pleasures of the table.

It has been said that it is impossible to watch a plant grow without getting a sense of the miracle of life. Use mealtimes to trace the food being eaten, from seed to plate. Explain the role of farms in the community food system, or for even more impact, grow your own vegetables and herbs. If you do not have a garden, herbs will thrive in containers, window boxes or hanging baskets, as long as there is adequate light and water.

Cooking classes can further nurture a love of fresh foods. Where possible, choose the classes that focus on seasonal, local foods with recipes that are simple to replicate at home. More information and ideas for stimulating a healthy appreciation of food can be gleaned from the ideals of the Slow Food movement (see www.slowfood.com).

Mother and daughter busy cooking dinner together.
OPPOSITE (FROM TOP): The Green School in Bali is built almost exclusively from sustainable, natural materials such as packed earth and bamboo; children developing their artistic creativity at the Green School.

THE SLOW HOME AND OFFICE

inspiring spaces

THE SLOW HOME AND OFFICE: INSPIRING SPACES

Nature is a difficult co-worker: She won't allow you to postpone things, and she is often ready for you when you aren't ready for her... [But] Nature, stern a mistress as she is, also wants to be loved.

- Joan Dye Gussow

Our ancestors created homes that were beautiful and ideally adapted to the local climate and built magnificent public structures that have withheld the test of time. Modern buildings, by comparison, are often soulless, mass-produced, poorly insulated, ill suited to the realities of the local climate and not built to last. These structures drain resources to heal and cool, to repair and, eventually, to rebuild.

However, the good news is that creating sustainable homes and workplaces has never been easier or more affordable. As environmental concerns are climbing to the top of the world's agenda and as consumers are demanding more sustainable homes, architects, planners, engineers and builders are rising to the challenge. Additionally, the choices of products on offer for the average individual or company are now much more extensive, with more options appearing on store shelves every day: where natural paint and FSC–certified wood were once hidden away in the most out of the way corners of the most remote hardware stores, these products are now commonplace in the best shops around the world; in most countries, domestic appliances come with an energy rating number or certification, designed to help consumers choose the most energy-efficient models; water-saving and reduced-flow devices for showers and taps are now commonplace; and when it comes to the softer touches such as textiles, with the range of colours and designs on offer, there is no excuse not to choose more sustainable, organic, natural and durable fabrics for your home. The workplace is no different: from computers, scanners, printers, desks, lighting, heating and air conditioning to smaller but equally important office essentials such as pens, stationery and personal organisers, a myriad of cleaner, sustainable options are on hand to improve the ecological footprints of every employee in every office.

Not too long ago, sustainable architecture and interior design was a hippy-style fringe movement. It is now at the cutting edge of design, and the challenge now is to ensure that this trend of best sustainable practice becomes normal practice—for every structure where we live and work.

Potted plants can help brighten the mood and clean the air at work.
OPPOSITE: Structures that exist in harmony with nature—like this pool villa at Soneva Kiri by Six Senses, Thailand—are now increasingly easy for individual homeowners to build and maintain.
PREVIOUS: A villa, at one with its environment, nestled in the green hillside at Six Senses Hideway Yao Noi, Thailand, at dawn.

The villas at Six Senses Hideaway Yao Noi, Thailand, are cooled by the shade of the nearby trees. OPPOSITE (FROM TOP): Natural ventilation and shade from overhanging roofs helps keep the temperature cool inside Six Senses Latitude Laamu, Maldives; ensuring that your home has good natural ventilation reduces the energy needed for air conditioning.

THE GREEN HOME The ideal home is a space that caters to our ever-changing moods. Balanced in every sense—physically, emotionally, functionally and spiritually—it is a space for living that meets our needs and does not harm our surroundings. With the sophistication of cutting-edge green design, you do not need to compromise on comfort or style when living in a sustainable home.

At its most basic level, a sustainable house is one that has a significantly lower impact on the environment than a standard building.

When building a new sustainable home, the key is firstly to reduce the amount of energy needed to construct the building by selecting materials like timber and clay that require little energy to extract and produce. Chemical finishes should be avoided, as these require larger amounts of energy to produce, while also releasing harmful fumes into the environment. The impact on the site should be kept to a minimum to help support existing biodiversity and reduce the need for intrusive energy-consuming works.

The next step is to consider how you will minimise the building's reliance on energy, once occupied. The best way of deciding how to make an existing home more energy efficient is by performing a home energy audit. By following simple guidelines, you can assess how much energy your home uses and what measures you can take to make it more efficient. Audits can be performed through reputable websites, such as the US Environmental Protection Agency (EPA) Energy Star programme (www.energystar.gov), or you can have a professional energy audit service perform a more thorough audit on your behalf.

CONSERVING ENERGY AT HOME

The use of electricity accounts for the bulk of energy consumption in our homes, and much of this energy is wasted. It has been estimated that for every kilowatt-hour used, 2.2 kilowatts are lost, as that energy is generated and sent over transmission lines. The infrastructure is inefficient and power hungry. Yet, even small changes in our habits can spark reductions in carbon emissions. For instance, if half of all light bulbs were switched to compact fluorescents, we could cut carbon emissions from lighting by 36 percent; and if all home computers were turned off when not in use, we could cut their impact by 50 percent (according to the Energy Information Administration, www.eia.doe.gov).

TEMPERATURE CONTROL According to the EPA, as much as half the energy used in the average household in the US goes to heating and cooling, so these are extremely important issues to consider when attempting to green your home. With a few simple steps, you can dramatically reduce energy consumption and bills at the same time. First,

properly insulate your home by implementing techniques such as sealing air leaks and placing insulating jackets on boilers. Then, make sure you choose only energy-efficient heating and cooling equipment. Replace old, wasteful equipment, as the energy savings of new models will mean lower electric bills that will help defray the cost of the purchase.

The electricity used for heating causes a huge percentage of our greenhouse emissions. One of the main reasons for this is that natural gas is a very common heating fuel. Essentially methane, this gas is the vapour equivalent of coal and oil, formed underground by decomposing matter over millions of years, making it unsustainable as an energy source.

REDUCING CARBON EMISSIONS FROM HEATING AND COOLING

It is possible to improve carbon emissions without completely changing your domestic heating and cooling systems by putting the following concepts into practise at home:

• Reducing heating and hot water temperatures by just a few degrees will significantly decrease the energy used.
• Keeping the hot water tank well insulated can reduce the energy required by between 25 and 45 percent.
• Heating or cooling only the rooms that are in use prevents wasting energy.
• Placing foil reflectors behind radiators ensures that the heat generated warms the room and not the walls.
• Drawing the curtains at dusk reduces the amount of heat escaping, which will reduce the heating needed at night.
• Using the principles of passive cooling, including maximising the effects of natural ventilation and shading, reduces the need for air conditioning.

Low-flow faucets, natural ventilation and energy-saving light bulbs come together in a beautiful, eco-friendly bathroom design at Six Senses Destination Spa-Phuket. OPPOSITE: Making your bathroom more environmentally friendly can be as simple as changing your shower head to a low-flow model.

ALTERNATIVE ENERGY SOURCES

If a truly sustainable home is the aim, then it is time to look to renewable energy sources. A fully sustainable home will incorporate a variety of clean energy systems, with the exact combination depending on the context of the project and the unique desires of the owners. However, whether the aim is to build a house from scratch or green up an existing building, numerous options are now available for every home and budget (see Chapter 1).

WATER At a time when climate change is causing droughts to occur more frequently in certain areas, water is becoming a very precious commodity. A series of dry winters

and hot summers and a generation of water-hungry appliances have compromised an already threatened water supply.

Research estimates that a family of four in the developed world uses approximately 200,000 litres (52,834 gallons) of water per year. The Centre for Alternative Technology (www.cat.org.uk) suggests that we should aim to reduce this astronomical figure by limiting our daily water use to about 80 litres (20 gallons) per person, and fortunately, this can be achieved without sacrificing your quality of life. You can make a big impact simply by using more energy-efficient fixtures and appliances, which will also mean significant savings on water and electricity bills. The following are some ideas to help conserve water and energy throughout the home:

• Water heaters: Ensuring the hot water tank is firmly insulated and turning down the thermostat by just a few degrees can significantly reduce heat loss.

• Taps: It is more economical to use a mixer tap that combines hot and cold water than two separate taps. Also, taps that work on a sensor will automatically switch off when there is nothing underneath them, thereby curtailing unnecessary water usage. Aerator and reduced flow models are also available. Aerators add air bubbles to the water to lessen water consumption. Reduced-flow models decrease water flow (and hence consumption) when the tap is turned on slightly and give full flow when the tap is turned on completely.

• Showers: A typical five-minute shower uses about 25 litres (7 gallons) of water, in comparison to 80 to 140 litres (20 to 37 gallons) for a bath and about 120 litres (32

gallons) for a power shower (in which a device is used to increase water pressure and therefore the amount of water propelled from the shower head). A simple way of decreasing water consumption is through low-flow shower heads that lessen water flow to 9.5 litres (3 gallons) per minute or less. Many new showers are automatically fitted with these low-flow heads, offering instant savings on water and heating bills. Digital showers can save water too, as long as they are used correctly. They are operated by a wireless remote control that signals when the shower is ready once a pre-set temperature and flow is reached. Flow is then decreased by half until someone gets in. But of course, you do not need fancy gadgets. Just limit your time in the shower, and turn off the water while washing hair.

- Toilets: Conventional toilets can flush as much as 13 litres (3 gallons) of water with every use. Dual flush toilets (which have separate settings for liquid and solid waste) and low-flow toilets can conserve a significant amount of water. Even replacing worn out toilet handles and tanks can save water. For those who are serious about saving the environment, a composting toilet is the best option (see www.composting toilet.org for further information).

- Watering the garden: Using a hose can consume more than 1,000 litres (264 gallons) of water per hour. By simply fitting a water butt (a receptacle that collects rainwater on the roof) to a pipe coming down to the garden, enough water can be accumulated to irrigate the garden and wash the car. Plants grow better with natural water too, making this an even more attractive option.

- Recycling and harvesting water: Grey water is water from showers, baths, washing machines, dishwashers and sinks. With some careful plumbing, it can be collected in a tank and reused to flush toilets and, in some cases, to water the garden (although it is not suitable for watering edible plants). Rainwater harvesting systems can reduce water consumption at home by up to half. A state-of-the-art system will include filters, pumps, storage tanks, an integrated rainwater-harvesting unit and environmentally friendly guttering, and this system can supply all domestic water needs, except for drinking water.

MY ECO LIFE
BY CHRISTINA DEAN, HONG KONG

"I'd never planned on being responsible. Neither did my plans include having children at the young age of 24 and moving to Hong Kong with a man I'd only just met.

My early twenties were defined by Ibiza in stilettos, Verbier in ski boots and Cape Town in platforms, grounded by my ill-conceived notion that I was the perfect match for planet earth because I loved life, and the world seemed to love me in return.

Like many romances, the realisation that things just weren't right hit suddenly, as I learned about the deaths associated with rising sea levels and increased droughts and floods. I soon realised that the environment was clearly better off without me. Feeling guilty about my carbon-intense lifestyle, I

gradually learned how to be more responsible. I've not exchanged my Jimmy Choos for gumboots, but I have taken the middle-ground approach to a more sustainable lifestyle and in the process am developing a new, responsible relationship with planet earth.

In doing so, many aspects of my family's lives have changed, starting in our home. Firstly, to give me some benchmark on my carbon footprint and to assess where most of my carbon contribution was coming from, I calculated my carbon footprint online via the Climate Friendly website (www.climatefriendly.com). This carbon calculator helps you to review your energy use and expenditure and provides an objective benchmark by which you can monitor your progress as you start unplugging. Hence, we have become misers with our electricity usage. I've stalked my husband (a passionate energy

consumer) and children around the house, making them turn lights off. We've amended our hot water timer and during the teething process endured many cold showers. The plugs for our enormous flat-screen plasma TV (a serious energy guzzler) and all its paraphernalia (sound boxes, dials and knobs) now plug into one multiple-plug extension lead, so we only need to unplug once to switch off its life support. The same was done for the computer, printer, router, mobile phone chargers and desk lights in the study.

Living in Hong Kong, air conditioning and dehumidifiers are a must for much of the year, unless one is happy to sweat uncomfortably and almost permanently. To maximise our appliances' efficiency, we washed or replaced the air filters in our air conditioners, removing foul clogged-up fluff.

Now the units run more efficiently and cleanly. Also, it goes without saying that in our quest to green up our home, we've changed our light bulbs from incandescent to compact fluorescent bulbs, which consume far less electricity. What astounded me was that over a period of just four months, our electricity bills decreased about 15 percent per month, without any significant impact on our lives—except a more positive bank balance. From electricity to water, our consumption has reduced dramatically.

We ditched our previous petrochemical detergents and now only use domestic products with plant-based ingredients that biodegrade back into the environment. This is a major domestic U-turn for me, since I was of the ilk that a bathroom is only clean if your eyes sting and your nose runs from the pungent smell of excess bleach. We also cut the number of weekly washes from six loads to three, and the tumble dryer is completely out of bounds except for medical or fashion emergencies.

The toilets now only know recycled toilet paper. My printer only knows recycled paper, which being heinously expensive has helped me reduce my printing. I've even taken the trouble to find places to recycle old print cartridges, and although this is much more time-consuming than simply binning them, I think that every little bit adds up.

I'm planning a new round of towel purchases and looking at either organic cotton or bamboo, both of which are far more sustainable than our present fabrics.

My clothing cupboards have mostly gone to charity. Believing that less is more, I am not buying so much 'stuff'. When I do buy, it's quality I choose over mass-produced quantity. I did, however, cough up top dollar for some fair-trade organic cotton jeans and some purple organic G-strings.

With grocery shopping, I am continuously moving towards more organic produce. Our bills are undoubtedly higher, but as Hong Kong is almost devoid of quality local produce, I am choosing top quality both for my family's health and for the pleasures of eating fresh, healthy food. I've also become a vegetarian along the way, as I know how unsustainable and destructive cattle farming and other intensive animal farming has become.

Another carbon disgrace that I discovered was my air travel. Because we're expats living on an island, some flights are unavoidable. The problem, of course, is that each flight quickly adds up, exceeding our supposed targets for annual carbon emission, and I love travelling! To ease my conscience somewhat, we now offset our carbon emissions from every flight, so at least I can fly with an easier mind.

My other carbon disgrace was a gas-guzzling Mercedes-Benz ML320. That's found a less green home, and I am now the proud owner of a Toyota Prius hybrid.

Is this quest to become more symbiotic with planet earth enough to impact climate change? I very much doubt that I alone will make an enormous difference. But I am hoping that I can entice others to join my journey. Now that I have equipped myself for a sustainable future, I've realised that loving life even more came as part of the deal."

FROM TOP: Recycling as much household waste as possible, including old newspapers, is an important step to greening your home; Christina Dean and family. OPPOSITE: Living in big cities like Hong Kong can reduce your carbon footprint, since homes are often smaller and make more efficient use of space.

Fans can reduce the need for air conditioning.
OPPOSITE (FROM LEFT): Insulating paints, when put on both interior and exterior walls, can dramatically reduce heating and cooling costs; using natural and unbleached cotton bathrobes and local, sustainable wood details are small eco-friendly touches that can be employed when outfitting a green bathroom.

GREEN MATERIALS Selecting eco-friendly materials when updating your existing home or when building a new one can make all the difference to your carbon footprint.
WOOD Wood is a natural, renewable, recyclable, biodegradable and non-toxic material that is more energy efficient to produce than most other hard materials. However, much of the wood that we see in furniture, floorboards and beds comes from disappearing rainforests, at a huge cost to the environment. Products made from trees that grow quickly, such as birch, beech and maple, for instance, are generally considered preferable. The best way of ensuring that the wood chosen is good and clean is to select products bearing the logo of the FSC. An international, independent non-profit organisation, the FSC only accredits wood when it can vouch for the entire supply chain—from the forest to the mill to the processor (see www.fsc-uk.org for more information). A well-maintained, FSC-certified timber floor will last for decades, and just as importantly, it also can be recycled or reused.

For those that prefer, durable and cost effective alternatives to wood are available in a range of styles and shades, including polished concrete; reclaimed or local stone (slate, limestone, flagstone, granite and marble); reclaimed tiles; cork; and rubber (both recycled rubber from tyres and natural rubber).
FLOOR COVERINGS When choosing a carpet, select from a wide variety of all-natural fibres (organic where possible) such as sea grass, hemp, jute and sisal—each having their own distinctive appearance and texture. They are available in a variety of weaves and patterns, and many can be naturally dyed. Linoleum flooring is another sustainable option. Manufactured from linseed oil, resin, wood flour or cork powder and pigments, linoleum is durable, scratchproof, easy to clean and waterproof, which makes it a perfect choice for bathrooms and kitchens.
PLASTER Clay plaster is a blend of fine aggregate and organic fibre that is easy to apply and additionally is a cost-effective and environmentally friendly alternative to cement-based plasters. It is stored as a dry powder to

which water is added. It then hardens after drying. The plaster remains workable for some time after application and can be reworked at any stage by simply adding water. It is also a more efficient heat regulator than cement, keeping walls cooler in summer and warmer in winter. Another option, lime plaster, comes as a powder of processed lime, water and aggregate that is easily mixed with water and can be coloured with natural pigments. It is compatible with many traditional and sustainable building materials, such as stone, straw bales and timber.

PAINT Paint can be a major indoor environmental hazard. Synthetic paints are made from petrochemical and mineral resources and release very high levels of VOCs into the air. These continue to be released months after the paint is applied, adding to atmospheric pollution and potentially causing health problems such as asthma, allergies and skin irritation. Many paint manufacturers now specify the VOC level on the tin.

In addition to VOCs, synthetic paint traditionally contains heavy metals, dyes and other chemicals that can accumulate in the body. While many are not definitively proven to be harmful as of yet, some are suspected to be toxic or carcinogenic. If buying synthetic paint, make sure to choose a zero-VOC, 100 percent-acrylic emulsion.

The healthiest paint option is natural paint free from VOCs or with greatly reduced levels of naturally occurring VOCs, such as pine resin or citrus-based solvent. In particular, look for oil-based emulsions, such as VOC-free linseed oil paints containing natural pigments, which are the kindest choice for the planet. Natural paints have a low embodied energy (i.e. the

energy and resources expended to make the product) and allow water to pass through without causing flaking or peeling. Plant resins and other materials used to make the paint repel dust and bacteria, unlike synthetic paint ingredients that are electrically charged and attract dust and bacteria. Also, most natural paints are totally biodegradable. The only drawback is that these paints are often more expensive and come in fewer colours than their synthetic alternatives. However, this is changing as more consumers demand healthier, more environmentally friendly paints.

INSULATING PAINTS

Insulating paints add an instant layer of insulation to walls. Made from insulating microspheres (tiny hollow ceramic balls), these paints were originally developed by NASA to combat the high temperatures that the space shuttle encounters when re-entering the atmosphere. These insulating paints have a non-conductive vacuum at the centre of their microspheres that reflects and refracts heat, so that when applied to internal walls and ceilings, the paint reduces heat loss, and when used on external walls and roofs, it helps to keep internal temperatures cooler.

FROM TOP: LED light bulbs come in a variety of sizes and shapes, and as they last longer than both incandscents and CFLs (and do not contain mercury), they are an ideal eco-friendly option; lighting decoration made entirely from local materials at Six Senses Destination Spa-Phuket.
OPPOSITE (FROM TOP): Guest bed with cotton net and bedding that is changed only when requested; locally-produced, naturally dyed, sustainable fabrics are used for the couches, chairs and daybeds in Six Senses Resorts & Spas.

WALLPAPER The ink that is traditionally used in wallpaper emits harmful VOCs, but natural or water-based choices are becoming more widely available. The most environmentally friendly wallpapers are those printed on recycled paper, sustainably produced wood pulp or natural plant fibres such as jute or sea grass. Water-soluble wallpaper pastes free from acrylic solvents, fungicides, preservatives and synthetic resins are also available but can be more expensive and harder to source.

LIGHTING Changing a light bulb can be the easiest and cheapest way of improving the environmental performance of a home. Traditional light bulbs account for up to 20 percent of domestic electricity usage and should be switched immediately in favour of one of the several types of energy-efficient light bulbs now available. Energy-efficient bulbs

last longer and consume less energy, thus saving money and reducing carbon emissions simultaneously—a win-win situation!

Among the most popular bulbs are:

- Compact fluorescent bulbs (CFLs): Consuming about 70 percent less energy than incandescent bulbs and lasting an average of 10 to 15 times longer, CFLs are especially useful in hotter climates as less heat is released as compared with incandescent bulbs. They come in a range of glows and fit most domestic sockets. The main problem with CFLs, like all fluorescent lamps, is that they contain mercury as vapour inside the glass tubing. This can further exacerbate air and water pollution. In view of this, many manufacturers have capped the amount of mercury that can be present in each bulb. Mercury is not as big of an issue in areas powered by coal because the CFLs can save on mercury emissions since less power will be used (as coal releases mercury as it burns). However, all CFLs, no matter where they are used, should be recycled rather than sent to a landfill.

- Halogen: These bulbs are particularly useful for smaller lights, modern track lighting and recessed wall lights. The best quality halogen bulbs last on average two to three times longer than a standard incandescent, burning at higher temperatures to give off a brighter light per watt.

- LED: Excellent for focus lights such as desk lamps, flashlights and reading lights, LED lights give off minimal heat and produce maximum light. Although they are the most expensive option, LEDs last an impressive 133 times longer than incandescent bulbs and about 10 times longer than a CFL bulb.

Dimmers are another efficient way of saving energy, while also extending the life of halogens or dimmer-compatible CFLs. Motion detectors are another option, which ensure that lights are only in use when needed. However, regardless of the bulb chosen and the various gadgets on offer, simply turning the lights off when you leave a room adds up to significant energy and financial savings.

KITCHEN UNITS If wood is your preferred material for kitchen cabinets, ensure it is FSC-certified. Skilled carpenters can make bespoke kitchen units to order, using sustainable FSC-certified wood. These units can be made watertight by rubbing natural oils or by coating them with environmentally friendly paint. Bamboo units, with their distinctive striped look, are growing in popularity and are now available in a range of styles. They are,

however, generally less hardwearing than wood and are more susceptible to scratches and dents. Other excellent alternatives include stone, metal, recycled plastic or glass worktops. Architectural salvage yards are great places for second-hand kitchen items, such as reclaimed slate worktops or Belfast sinks.

TEXTILES Domestic fabric is traditionally full of chemicals such as dioxins, flame retardants and chlorine bleach. Not only do these emit toxins in the home, but they also contribute to pollution of the outside environment during both their manufacture and disposal. Natural fabrics such as organic cotton, linen and silk are rapidly gaining popularity in homes throughout the world. Cork, bamboo, soya and tree bark are other options, as is hemp, a highly versatile fabric that can be made into a range of products, including shower curtains and sofa

FROM TOP: Designers are using recycled woods—like the driftwood used to make this unique bench at Soneva Fushi, Maldives—to create cutting-edge furniture; dresser made entirely from sustainable materials.
OPPOSITE (FROM TOP): Clothes drying in the sun at a Six Senses resort; to save energy, make sure to use a front-loading washing machine set at a low temperature.

covers. Sustainable fabrics use a combination of renewable resources, including low-energy and clean production processes, safe chemicals and dyes and biodegradable or recyclable materials.

The best way to find sustainable or recycled fabric is through specialised eco stores or via the Internet. It is advisable to check the origin of the fabric before purchasing it. Fabric made from pesticide-free crops will be non-toxic and healthier for the home. In addition, recycling and reusing fabric reduces the material that would be lost to the landfill, while also saving the energy and resources that would have been used to create new products. Moreover, in terms of creating an original look for your home, sustainable fabric is rarely mass-produced, giving interior designs that unique twist.

FURNITURE Creative furniture designers are pushing the boundaries of sustainable design inventing chic new objects from recycled woods, glass and plastics. Furniture made from renewable materials (e.g. bamboo and timber) is readily available too. Even better, reusing an antique dining or dressing table or a chandelier from the skip saves the energy needed to manufacture a new item and the waste caused by dumping the old.

APPLIANCES

A large proportion of household power is simply wasted by inefficient fridges, overfilled kettles and TVs and computers left on standby. Making more efficient choices when equipping a kitchen can hugely impact a home's overall energy consumption. There is no excuse not to do so, as energy-saving appliances now sit next to conventional models in almost all hardware and specialist stores. While some of these appliances may cost more upfront, most will eventually prove to be the more economical choice, by saving energy and hence money from bills. When choosing a model, do your research to choose the energy-saving logo appropriate for your country.

OVENS A fan-assisted oven heats up 30 times faster than a conventional model, consuming far less energy. Gas hobs and ovens use half the energy of traditional electric models. Induction hobs are the most efficient of all as they generate heat very quickly. Some will even turn off automatically when a pot is removed from the burner.

HOUSEHOLD FRIDGES AND FREEZERS Collectively responsible for about one-third of domestic appliance energy use in the home, refrigerators and freezers run continuously. So, if you have an old and inefficient model, seriously consider upgrading. It will save energy from the moment it is plugged in and pay for itself within a few years. Regularly check that the seal is working efficiently by shutting the door on a piece of paper. Also, remember that fridges positioned close to heat sources can take up to 15 percent more energy to run. And finally, a well-stocked fridge uses less energy than an empty one.

DISHWASHERS Since generating heat is the big energy drain for dishwashers, run your machine on the coolest setting (and when buying a new model, look for those that offer low settings). Also, use plant-based detergent.

WASHING MACHINES AND DRYERS It is gauged that about 90 percent of the energy expended in washing clothes is consumed in heating the water. Hot water is not essential in washing. In fact, colours will stay

intact longer with cold water cycles, which are better for fibres as they cause less heat damage. Choose more energy-efficient washing machines and wash clothes at the lowest temperature possible—often 30°C (86°F).

Front-loading washing machines are far more energy efficient than top loaders. They consume about half the amount of water as top-loading machines, and less detergent is required, as a much smaller amount of soapy water is needed when clothes are tumbled around sideways in a front-loading machine, as opposed to being soaked in the deep tub of a top-loading model. As front loaders spin faster, they extract more water, which means less drying time and less wear and tear on clothes.

Dryers are massive energy consumers and polluters. Drip-drying clothes on a drying rack or clothing line in the sunshine is the most obvious eco-friendly option. Not only will clothes smell fresher, it may also make them cleaner naturally; the sun's ultraviolet rays are thought to have inherent anti-bacterial properties. However, if a dryer is absolutely necessary, just give air-dried clothes a very quick spin, when they are almost dry.

LAUNDRY DETERGENTS

Most traditional laundry products contain synthetic perfumes, which are made of chemicals that are linked to cancer and reproductive abnormalities. Fragrances and other synthetic additives can also cause skin irritation and other allergic reactions.

Healthier detergents are obtainable, but many people are uncertain of their cleaning efficiency when compared with their synthetic predecessors. While it depends on the product in question, most of these biodegradable eco-brands contain non-toxic solvents, natural enzyme stain removers and biodegradable ingredients that are equally effective for general day-to-day cleaning. Also, to give your clothes that extra bright look, you can put them in the washer with water for a pre-soak before starting the machine's cycle.

In truth, you can almost get by with no washing powder at all as sweat and the most common types of dirt are water soluble and can be removed by warm water and the rotating action of a washing machine—hence the success of eco-balls and eco-discs, which claim to eliminate the need for detergents by ionising or magnetising the water. Devotees swear by the clean, fresh natural smell and claim no difference in cleaning effectiveness.

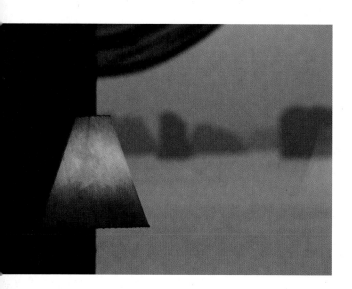

CHEMICAL- AND TOXIN-FREE CLEANING AT HOME

Try the following natural cleaning alternatives instead of synthetic products that may bring toxins into your home:

- Tea tree oil is a natural disinfectant. Add a few drops to hot water for cleaning kitchen or bathroom surfaces.
- Baking soda helps remove stains. It can help clean the fridge, tiles and jewellery.
- Lemon juice is an effective, natural substitute for bleach.
- White wine vinegar, when a teaspoon is added to a bucket of hot water, gives windows and glass a great shine, while also removing mould. It is a stain remover too.
- Borax or white vinegar acts as a natural fabric conditioner when one-quarter cup is added during the last rinse.
- Essential oils such as lavender, rose or eucalyptus can add a pleasant scent to clean laundry. If you miss the aroma of synthetic perfumes, just add a few drops to each wash.

TVS, DVDS AND STEREOS It is estimated that 8 percent of domestic electricity is consumed by appliances such as TVs, DVDs, stereos and computers left on standby. The proliferation of over-sized televisions alone can offset any gains made elsewhere. Some of the worst offenders are flat-screen plasma TVs that typically use four times the energy of the older models. If buying one, consider an integrated digital television, as it saves energy by using only one power socket and standby circuit.

As manufacturers strive to create more energy-efficient appliances, standby buttons are gradually being phased out. Consumers can take the responsibility into their own hands as well by getting into the habit of turning off devices properly when not in use. This can save on emissions and bills.

POWERING DOWN IN THE HOME
Making these simple changes will reduce energy costs considerably:

- Only buy approved appliances bearing energy certification or energy rating labels (e.g. the US EPA-approved Energy Star Program and the EU Energy Label).
- Protect windows from the sun's rays with large overhangs and double-pane glass.

- Turn off lights, fans, air conditioners and appliances when they are not needed.
- Use energy-efficient light bulbs.
- Control heat, air and moisture leakage by sealing windows and doors.
- Insulate the attic and basement with natural, non-toxic materials.
- Use renewable energy sources, such as solar electric systems, compact wind turbines, geothermal heat pumps, etc.
- Be conscious of conserving water, using it only as needed.
- Limit the amount of clothes that are washed.
- Only use the washing machine when it is fully loaded, and remember that most clothes can be worn more than once before being tossed into the laundry.
- Dry clothes the natural way—on a clothesline. Limit using the dryer to emergencies only.
- Recycle everything you can. Most waste can be recycled: waste paper becomes newspaper; glass bottles become insulation; and fruit peel becomes earth.
- Reduce paper use by printing less and paying bills online, which saves trees and envelopes, while also eliminating the fuel required to transport the mail.
- Use rechargeable batteries.
- Consider the benefits of living in a city. High-rise apartment blocks can be more sustainable, as spaces tend to be smaller. The denser the area you call home, the smaller your carbon footprint.
- Say no to plastic bags. Use bags made of cloth or other biodegradable material.
- Shop with a conscience. Be more aware of each product's lifecycle, and see how you can sensibly reduce waste.

THE ECO-VILLA

The Eco-Villa is a zero-carbon-emissions suite at Soneva Kiri by Six Senses on Koh Kood, Thailand. It showcases a range of experimental environmental technologies incorporated into a bio-climatically designed luxury pool villa, which was built to demonstrate that, even on the remotest of islands, the best of comfort and convenience can be enjoyed while treading very lightly on the earth.

The Eco-Villa was constructed from locally sourced building materials by a team of highly skilled local Thai craftsmen, including mud brick experts, terracotta potters, master carpenters and stonemasons, who used a combination of modern building design and state-of-the-art, zero-carbon-emissions, clean-energy technology combined with indigenous skills and knowledge.

Low-embodied-energy materials, recycled waste products and green building techniques were used throughout the construction. Key building features include the use of local sandstone; rice husks; soil and straw for the walls; harvested, kiln-dried and treated timber; FSC-certified pine and reclaimed teak for the ceiling, floors and fittings. Recycled egg crates were used in the drainage layer of the green roof, and soda bottles found a new life as glass bricks in the shower.

Other features include driftwood beds, canvas ceiling fans, solar powered electricity and air conditioning, a natural rainwater-filtered swimming pool, a rainwater collection and harvesting system, a wine cellar and a sturdy bamboo spaceship hammock made from rattan and leaves with a soft rubber mattress. Light emanates from a central skylight that is perfect for viewing the stars at night.

The Eco-Villa's energy needs are met via a hybrid system of clean renewable energy, comprising a wind turbine, photovoltaic solar panels and a micro-hydro system using wastewater from the restaurant located above the villa.

The landscaping is an eclectic blend of endemic, adapted plants and organic, edible plants and herbs. Much of the existing vegetation was preserved, and any trees that could have been harmed during the construction of the Eco-Villa were temporarily moved to a nursery and then replanted on site.

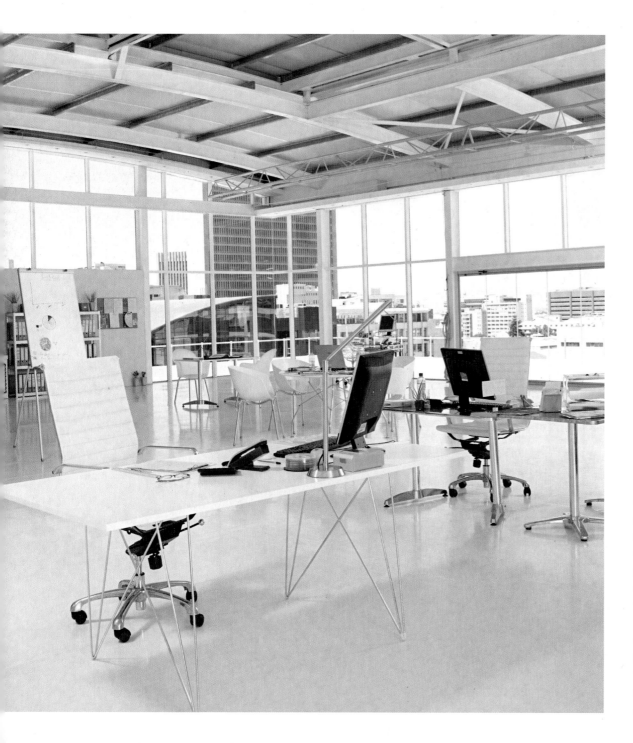

CONSERVING ENERGY IN THE WORKPLACE

In an ideal world, we would work with companies for whom renewable energy is a given—companies that grow their own organic vegetables, use only credited energy-efficient appliances, offer bicycle parking and who reimburse employees for purchasing energy-efficient cars. In reality, the vast majority of us do not. However, there are simple changes that can be made in the office that will contribute significantly to our health and that of the planet. Businesses do not reduce power consumption—people do. Bringing good habits from home to the office and sharing them with colleagues and friends saves money, energy and the planet.

A WASTE AUDIT Whether you work on a farm, from home or in a large corporation, you can streamline business operations, save money and help clean up the environment by simply conducting a waste audit and acting on the results.

Start by taking visual stock of what is normally thrown out and what is recycled (e.g. paper, printer cartridges, cans, plastics and packing materials). This will help you to identify opportunities to reduce materials used and give more products a new life through recycling (paper, containers, toner cartridges and cardboard are excellent candidates for recycling). Share your findings with your colleagues and prove to the management that going green can save money.

PAPER Paper made from virgin wood contributes massively to deforestation by reducing both the number of trees available for absorbing carbon and by releasing the carbon contained in the felled trees. According to US-based environmental advocacy group Natural Resources Defense Council (www.nrdc.org), the average office worker discards about 160 kg (350 lbs) of paper per year. Much of this can be saved. Think twice before printing, make double-sided copies and use scrap paper where possible. Choosing a type of paper with a high post-consumer recycled content (made with materials recovered from those previously used by consumers) diverts waste from landfills and helps to create demand for recycled products. OFFICE EQUIPMENT If you are in charge of buying equipment for your office, then ensure that only energy-saving printers, copiers, scanners and fax machines, which use about half as much electricity as standard equipment, are bought. Recycling bins for paper, cardboard and reusable necessities such as plates and cups are other green office essentials. Suggest that your company purchase its power from renewable sources and install motion sensors for lighting. If you work in a place where these decisions are out of your control, lobby your colleagues and managers to take these initiatives. COMPUTERS With computer life spans shrinking as we load them up, wear them out and turn to ever-faster processing power, more non-biodegradable, polluting merchandise is sent to landfills every year. Additionally, keeping the world connected 24/7 requires massive amounts of energy. The average desktop computer, for instance, consumes between 80 and 250 watts (laptops consume about 30 to 80 watts) per hour.

To keep your computer functioning at maximum efficiency, adjust the power options in the control panel to energy-saving settings. Screen savers consume as much electricity as an idle computer. Using the sleep mode function can reduce energy consumption by up to 70 percent. Always turn computers off overnight or when not in use for an extended period of time. Shutting the system down completely will not wear your computer out, rather it will help conserve energy, reduce mechanical stress and prolong the computer's life, while cutting electricity bills in the process.

When purchasing a new computer, ensure it meets Electronic Product Environmental Assessment Tool (EPEAT) standards (www.epeat.net). EPEAT rates computers on their raw materials, end-of-life design, longevity, packaging and many other qualities relating to their construction and overall performance. Also, check that your computer meets with the European Union's Restriction of Hazardous Substances (www.rohs.eu) requirements or the equivalent in other markets. Many of the larger computer manufacturers make energy-efficient PCs with reduced amounts of mercury, cadmium, lead and other hazardous substances, which makes disposing of the computer less of an environmental concern.

Look out for computer casings made from bamboo and other recyclable or renewable materials. Efficient solar power for laptops are available too, in the form of portable and easily chargeable solar-powered backpacks.

Limiting time spent on the computer is not only good for the environment, but it may also be good for your health. Placing laptops directly on the lap has been linked to health concerns such as a decrease in fertility for men. Also, make sure to turn off Wi-Fi Internet when not in use, as some studies suggest that continued exposure to Wi-Fi is unhealthy.

FROM TOP: Guest information folders, made from naturally dyed recycled paper at Six Senses Resorts & Spas; a recycled paper notebook with a pencil set created from non-toxic and sustainable materials. OPPOSITE: Switching computers off when not in use is crucial to conserving energy at work. PREVIOUS (FROM LEFT): The Eco-Villa at Soneva Kiri by Six Senses, Thailand; the Eco-Villa's daybed, made from bamboo.

SICK BUILDING SYNDROME If you suffer from constant sneezing, stuffy or runny nose, headache, dry mucous membranes and a debilitating lack of energy, this may be caused by indoor air pollution and toxic building design. Efficient design, operation and maintenance of a building's ventilation system are a prerequisite for employee health and productivity, an issue that is all too often ignored by companies.

If you cannot initiate changes in your office alone, then lobby colleagues and relevant management to clean up the office, in order to make it a safer and more productive environment for everyone.

WORKING FROM YOUR HOME
Video conferencing, instant messaging and online chat forums make telecommuting from home a real possibility. If you can work from home, do. From a practical perspective alone, it will cut out the commute, reduce paper and energy use and leave you in full control of your working life. Chances are you will be happier and more productive than when you were working in an office. The following are a few guidelines to get you started:

- Choose a workspace: Setting aside a space dedicated only to work helps you stay focused. Find a space that inspires you, with big windows and plenty of sunlight.

- Find a desk: Think carefully about what kind of desk you want and have space for. When you decide the style, make sure it is made from FSC-certified wood, recycled metal with non-toxic finishes or purchased from antique stores, thrift shops or yard sales.

- Get connected: Along with an efficient computer, you will probably need a mobile phone, scanner, printer and fax machine,

depending on the type of work you do. Research the energy ratings of these appliances online to ensure that you buy the cleanest and most efficient model with the least environmental impact.

- Smart accessories: Buy only recycled paper, pencils made from sustainable wood or old denim, rechargeable batteries and other cleaner accessories. Use electronic invoices and online payments for all accounts.
- Co-working: Shared office spaces where freelancers and other self-employed people jointly rent office space are becoming more and more popular. If you do not have the space to work from home or prefer to work alongside others, then check out what is available in your area.

POWERING DOWN AT WORK

There are many ways of reducing your carbon emissions in the office, from the products you buy to the way you approach printing and to the companies you hire for services. Try some of these easy ways to implement green tactics:

- Save paper and power by sending e-mails rather than a fax.
- Use reusable containers and utensils if bringing lunch to work. If an order is being placed to have food delivered, then join in with colleagues and make it a larger, more efficient order.
- Use the stairs when possible. It is better for your health and for the environment.
- Reuse all paper in the office for double-sided printing or to make scribbling pads.
- Check documents carefully with the print preview function before printing to avoid having to reprint unnecessarily.
- Print only when absolutely necessary.

- Use potted plants to help brighten the office mood and to reduce the carbon dioxide in the atmosphere.
- Increase the thermostat of the office air conditioning system. An increase of just a few degrees can make a large contribution to limiting electricity consumption.
- Walk, run or cycle when commuting to work. Your commute can become an effective weekday workout.
- Use public transport to commute, or if feasible, start a car pool with co-workers. Sharing a ride just twice a week reduces carbon dioxide output significantly.
- Limit the use of staples. Some studies claim that if every office worker used one less staple a day, we could save more than 100 tonnes of steel per year.
- Try to implement Earth Hour—a time when electrical gadgets are switched off—every day, week or month.
- Remember that screen savers save computer screens, not energy. Starting up and shutting down your computer do not use extra energy, nor are they hard on computer components. In fact, shutting computers down regularly actually reduces system wear, and it saves a substantial amount of energy over the long term.
- Make your printer's toner last as long as possible. Change the printer settings to economy mode when printing drafts or documents for internal use. Economy mode uses up to 50 percent less toner and prints twice as many pages, as compared to higher quality settings.
- Look for penholders, paper files, envelopes and computers made from bamboo or other sustainable materials.

FROM TOP: Homemade vegetable soup in a Thermos flask—the perfect reusable container—is a nutritious and eco-friendly lunch option for the office; taking the stairs instead of the elevator is good for you and the environment. OPPOSITE: Working from home eliminates the need for a daily commute.

SLOW TRAVEL
fun adventures

SLOW TRAVEL: FUN ADVENTURES

The industry as a whole now needs to design, develop, refurbish and operate a new generation of tourism destinations that have a minimum ecological footprint and which also support and strengthen the communities in which they operate.

- HRH The Prince of Wales, President, The International Business Leaders Forum and Founder, International Tourism Partnership

There are few places left on earth that cannot be reached by tourists eager to explore the final frontiers. According to the UN World Tourism Organization, the number of international trips made each year exceeds 900 million and is anticipated to reach one billion by 2010.

High speed international travel is an essential part of globalisation and makes the modern world work. Life without the car, airplane, hotel and restaurant is hard to imagine. Yet, life with many of today's accessories is proving difficult to sustain. Consequently, the tide is turning as a new wave of sophisticated, savvy travellers are seeking authentic destinations, where nature remains king, where "environmental consciousness" and "sustainability" are more than just words, and where the wellbeing of the earth and its inhabitants takes precedence.

Tourism can provide the perfect incentive for countries to look after their environments. If tourists visit to see pristine landscapes and animals in their native wild homes, these features become valuable assets worth protecting, offering a challenging but more humane alternative to such damaging industries as tree felling and prostitution. This is especially important in developing markets, where tourist dollars are the main source of income.

Changing climatic conditions and extreme events are affecting tourism operations in many ways—from transport disruptions and reduced freshwater resources to the degradation of natural landscapes, marine habitats and wildlife populations. As ecosystems suffer and struggle to adapt, the tourism sector must acclimatise by becoming more accountable and realise that sound environmental management makes good business sense. Just as the SLOW way of eating asks diners to savour meals and appreciate the way food is produced, SLOW travel promotes a more thoughtful and meaningful style of travel, while also offering a path for discovering unforgettable experiences.

The sophisticated interior of Manned Cloud Airship, an exciting innovation in eco-friendly travel, will have all the amenities of a cruise ship. Fuel-efficient and limiting the need for hotels, this unique concept could allow passengers to experience exotic places without being overly intrusive or exploitative, when it launches in 2020. OPPOSITE: A romantic dinner for two is served in a tent surrounded by the ocean at Soneva Fushi by Six Senses, Maldives, at twilight. PREVIOUS: Shadow of an airplane flying over an African landscape dotted with elephants.

Traffic whizzing by on a busy motorway in Scotland.
OPPOSITE (FROM TOP):
Merchants paddling through Bangkok's Floating Market, selling their freshly picked produce;
a polar bear's tracks in the snow across the tundra in Kaktovik, Alaska.

SUSTAINABLE TOURISM

Responsible travel is not new. Eco–tourism first emerged in the 1970s in response to the destruction of the Amazon rainforest and poaching in Africa. From these initial efforts that introduced the concept of low-impact and conservation-driven holiday making, a more responsible industry is maturing—one that is touching the hearts of an increasing number of travellers.

What is new, on the other hand, is the rise in volunteerism and philanthropic travel, in which travellers actively support environmental conservation, cultural heritage and economic development initiatives. From tracking the last rhinos in Borneo and saving the African elephant to building schools, homes, mini-water sanitation foundations and wind turbines, travellers are focusing less on monuments and more on the unexpected treasures as they make real connections with the community and environments that they visit.

Travellers are realising that there is more to being a responsible citizen than monitoring carbon footprints, and rather than exploiting their host country's heritage, environment and people, they are contributing to its progress. Notable travel operators and resorts, especially in wild, unspoiled landscapes, are inviting their guests to become part of this change.

TRANSPORT Each of the many modes of travelling the earth take their toll on the planet. However, technological innovations and smarter choices made by individuals can reduce carbon emissions dramatically.
AVIATION Since the Wright brothers first revealed the potential of powered flight more than one century ago, the skies have opened, aircrafts have become more sophisticated and people are travelling more frequently. According to the Intergovernmental Panel on Climate Change, aviation accounts for between 3 and 4 percent of the total human impact on climate change.

Although some of this is due to the overall distance travelled, more of it seems to relate to how the planes fly and the vapour trails they create. Aircraft emissions are compounded in the sky's upper trophosphere and lower stratosphere, where planes spend the majority of their flying time. Planes also leave a trail of carbon dioxide, nitrogen oxide and other pollutants in their wake.

Added to this are the contrails (or vapour trails) created by aircraft at high altitudes. Researchers believe that these visible line clouds that form in cold, humid atmospheres compound the global warming effect. The persistent formation of contrails gives rise to cirrus clouds (high clouds that consist of ice particles) that can trap and reflect heat beneath them. The clouds have a global warming effect over and above that of

contrail formation alone. Most estimates of aviation's effect on climate change do not account for the cirrus cloud effect, meaning that the impact of air travel is in fact more significant than many current statistics suggest.

New aviation concepts and fuel alternatives are pushing the boundaries of flying, offering the potential for significant carbon savings throughout the industry. Innovations ranging from solar airplanes running exclusively on synthetic jet fuel, turbine engine-powered short-haul airlines, airships and very light jets (VLJs), to cutting-edge advances in fuel cell and lithium-ion battery technology, all give plenty of reason for optimism for a cleaner, more sustainable future.

While there is no doubt that innovative aircraft like these will eventually emerge, they are a long way off and will not replace current

In a more cacophonous, relentlessly always on world, people will look for sanctuary: pockets of calm and breathing spaces where they can be themselves. What many rushed, stressed people want more than anything else is a bit of time. In a world that seems to worship speed going a little faster is not a luxury. Being able to go a lot slower is the luxury. That is what we envy.

- Charles Leadbeater, www.charlesleadbeater.net

fleets immediately, since passenger planes stay in use for decades. For now, experts insist that governments and the airline industry need to focus more on increasing the efficiency of existing aircraft systems and searching for more realistic fuel alternatives. Fortunately, there are a number of lower-tech innovations that are delivering emissions reductions here and now. Among the easiest and possibly most effective are those that require little or no technology— such as a change in flying behaviour. For example, landing jumbo jets in idle and reducing aircraft speed saves on fuel, as does selecting more direct routes.

For the traveller, cutting back on air travel is an obvious solution. This might mean giving up flying all together, flying less and staying longer or choosing destinations closer to home.

If you choose to fly, consider offsetting your emissions (see page 25). Also, check out which airlines are actively working to improve their emissions or donate a percentage of profits to charitable projects. For domestic and trans-

continental travel, trains are becoming the preferred mode of transport (where they are available). They are estimated to emit 10 times less carbon dioxide than planes, while also being convenient for passengers, as there is little security screening and fewer delays.

CARS As yet, there is no such thing as a truly ecologically friendly automobile, but there are cleaner choices available. The type of car we choose, the fuel we buy and the manner in which we drive can make for a healthier, more sustainable planet.

The US EPA report "Transportation Greenhouse Gas Emissions 1990–2003" found that light-duty vehicles such as cars, vans, minivans and pickup trucks accounted for 62 percent of all greenhouse gas emissions caused by transportation in the US. Passenger cars alone are responsible for 35 percent of this, the largest contributor of any vehicle category, above heavy-duty vehicles and aircraft. Car emissions include a cocktail of carcinogens and noxious fumes that, according to many sources, are largely responsible for the health burdens associated with airborne pollution.

Much can be done to reduce this toxic burden. Even if you drive a fuel-guzzling car, you can reduce its fuel usage by up to 30 percent by tweaking regular driving practices:

- Drive at the right speed: Most cars achieve maximum fuel efficiency when travelling at speeds of around 50–70 km per hour (30–40 miles per hour). As speeds edge above 80 km per hour (50 miles per hour), fuel consumption increases by as much as 15 percent for every additional 10 km per hour (6 miles per hour).
- Lighten the load: Adding an extra 45 kg (100 lb) in your car reduces fuel economy by up to 2 percent.
- Use the boot: Placing luggage inside the car, rather than on the roof, minimises drag and increases fuel efficiency.
- Keep tyres properly inflated: Less surface area coming in contact with the road equates to less drag and more efficiency.
- Visit your mechanic: Tuning the engine regularly keeps the car running efficiently.
- Avoid idling, except when necessary: Every five minutes of idling emits about 500 gm (1 lb) of greenhouses gases into the air.
- Minimise starting and stopping: Accelerate gradually and anticipate stops. Starting and stopping increases wear and tear on the car and also drains fuel economy.
- Reduce air conditioning: If the outside temperature is comfortable, use the vents and fan and leave the air conditioning off.

TIPS FOR MORE SUSTAINABLE TRAVEL

- Take fewer flights, and enjoy longer trips.
- Deal only with reputable and responsible travel companies.
- When making travel arrangements choose overland where possible, preferably using public transport (e.g bus or train).
- Before leaving home, unplug all appropriate electronics and adjust your home's heating and cooling systems and water thermostat in order to save energy.
- If staying in a hotel, turn off air conditioning, lights and TV when leaving the hotel room, and let housekeeping know that you do not need your bed linen and towels changed daily.
- Use reusable containers for toiletries.
- Do not bring your plastic rubbish with you. If you do, dispose of it sensibly, or bring it back home with you where it can be recycled.
- To save paper, take brochures and maps only if absolutely needed.
- Do not buy products that you suspect are made from endangered animal parts, such as tortoise shell, ivory, *shahtoosh*, skins and feathers. Seashells and other marine life are generally questionable.
- Do not collect souvenirs from wild areas as this could disrupt the ecosystem.
- Remember sustainability means doing things better—not doing without.

ELECTRIC CARS Electric cars are presently the cleanest vehicles on four wheels. Running explicitly on batteries, they generate zero emissions while on the go. Like most battery-powered devices, they have no harmful emissions, and if charged with electricity from clean renewable sources, their use creates practically no carbon dioxide. Even if charged with electricity generated from fossil fuels, they are still more energy-efficient than petrol cars. The downside is that most electric cars on the market do not travel fast and regularly need to be parked beside a plug socket to recharge. These sockets are still rare in many parts of the world and recharging can be a lengthy process. Also, the batteries used need to be replaced, resulting in toxic waste.

ELECTRIC HYBRID CARS Electric hybrid cars look and drive like normal cars, yet they are semi-electric. Unlike true electric cars, hybrids do not need to be plugged in to recharge. Instead, the car charges its own battery when the brakes are applied and when the petrol–powered part of the engine is commanding the car at high speeds. The battery's energy is used automatically at lower speeds. A technique called pulse-and-glide driving—hovering at optimal speed range by making small changes in speed—can further boost a hybrid's efficiency.

The main drawback with hybrids at present is their cost, which can be up to 20 percent more than an equivalent non-hybrid model when purchased new. In some bigger cities like London, for example, they are exempt from congestion charges, so some savings can be made. Also, much of the hybrid's efficiency rests in the style of driving. At lower speeds using the pulse-and-glide technique over

Although cars are becoming more sustainable with respect to both their fuel efficiency and their emissions of toxic greenhouse gases, some are better than others. If you are buying a car, seek out the lowest emissions model that fits your needs and budget. Even if it means spending more upfront, you will most likely save money in the long run due to reduced fuel costs. Smaller, lighter cars are best, in general, as they consume less fuel. Also, there are more vehicles benefiting from new technology aimed at reducing environmental impact. For instance, there are three main types of electric vehicles—those running strictly on batteries (electric), hybrid petrol-electric vehicles (hybrids) and fuel-cell vehicles.

shorter distances, hybrids are indeed cleaner, but when driven over long distances at high speeds, this is not the case. Having two engines, hybrid cars tend to be heavier and less efficient. Also, as with electric cars, the batteries need replacing, resulting in toxic waste when they are thrown away.

FUEL-CELL CARS Fuel-cell cars use a device that converts hydrogen and oxygen directly into electrical energy to power the motor and propel the vehicle. Like electric cars, fuel-cell vehicles result in significantly reduced air-borne pollution (water vapour is often the only emission), and they can be extremely efficient. Hydrogen-driven buses and taxis are currently in experimental use in some larger cities and have resulted in significantly reduced emissions.

Although hydrogen is plentiful, clean and transportable, it has some drawbacks, including the fact that the atom is highly combustible, difficult to confine and expensive to harness. Additionally, the fuel cells are incredibly fragile, very costly to produce and a lot of energy (primarily derived from fossil fuels) is required to separate the hydrogen and oxygen in water. For hydrogen to become a realistic renewable energy source, further research is still required.

COMPRESSED AIR CARS Instead of mixing fuel with air and burning it to drive the piston, compressed air cars use the expansion of compressed air to drive their pistons. This idea is not new. Early prototypes of an air-powered vehicle go back to the middle of the

Not always sluggish and geeky-looking, some of the more recent models of electric cars adapt the look and speed of traditional sports cars, accelerating from 0 to 97 km per hour (0 to 60 miles per hour), in as little as 2.5 seconds.
OPPOSITE (FROM TOP): A charging station for electric cars in Arizona, US; a young woman charging her electric car at a socket on the street in London, UK.

Interior of the cutting-edge hydrogen-powered 2007 Hyundai i-Blue fuel-cell car. OPPOSITE: Jars filled with different stages of the production of biodiesel on display at the first National Sustainable Design Expo in Washington, DC, in 2006.

19th century, even before the invention of the internal combustion engine. But it is only more recently that the prospect of cost-effective mass production has become a possibility. These high-tech wonders have no keys—just an access card that is read from your pocket.

Compressed-air cars are emission-free at the tailpipe. Since its source of energy is usually electricity, its total environmental impact depends on how clean the electricity source is. Few pollutants are emitted, mainly just dust from the brakes and tyre wear. Also, it is very cost-efficient to run (estimated to be about one-tenth the cost of a petrol car), and its mileage is about double that of the most advanced electric car on the market, making it a perfect choice for city driving. Tests have found that the cars have a top speed of about 110 km per hour (68 miles per hour) on highways with a general range of 80 km per

hour (50 miles per hour). Refilling can take place using a home air compressor or, if the market develops, at petrol stations that have been adapted to administer compressed air.

Like the modern car and most household appliances, their principal disadvantage is the indirect use of energy. For compressed-air cars, energy is lost when electrical energy is converted to compressed air. Additionally, refuelling in the home is a lengthy process.

DRIVING LESS The cleanest, most effective method of improving your environmental impact is to drive less. To this end, car sharing is becoming a popular option, based on the rationale that one car carrying three people is three times better than three cars carrying one person each. People can check the Internet for other like-minded commuters, which is especially helpful in areas where public transport is not readily available.

CLEANER FUEL

Petrol (gasoline) and diesel are still the main fuel for vehicles in most parts of the world. Although standard diesel emits far more poisonous chemicals than petrol engines, diesel engines are significantly more fuel efficient, especially when used in the countryside.

DIESEL ALTERNATIVES

Biodiesel refers to a non-petrolatum-based diesel fuel made by chemically reacting lipids (typically vegetable oil or animal fat) and alcohol. It can be used on its own or blended with conventional diesel in most vehicles with little to no modification. Both virgin and waste oil (often collected from restaurants) can be used with equally good results. The fuel can be produced domestically from seed to pump and is non-toxic and biodegradable. Biodiesel typically produces about 60 percent less net carbon dioxide emissions than standard diesel, while reducing the amount of exhaust fumes (e.g. carbon monoxide).

The main problem with much of the biodiesel now in use is that it often comes from palm oil, and the planting of palm oil plantations has caused widespread deforestation and carbon emissions, in Asia in particular, negating any perceived benefits.

From a practical perspective, biodiesel is known to become slightly gelatinous at low temperatures and is therefore not suitable for year-round use in some climates. This can be addressed by using blends of biodiesel with conventional hydrocarbon diesel that are being sold in a growing network of filling stations in major cities. Much of the world uses a system known as the "B" factor to state the amount of biodiesel in any fuel mix. For example, blends of 20 percent biodiesel with 80 percent petroleum diesel (B20) can generally be used in unmodified diesel engines, while biodiesel in its pure form (B100) may require certain engine modifications for ideal performance.

GASOLINE ALTERNATIVES

The use of pure alcohol (ethanol) in internal combustion engines is only possible if the engine is designed or modified for that purpose. It can,

however, be mixed with gasoline in various ratios for use in unmodified engines, and with minor modifications, engines can use fuel with a higher content of ethanol. Ethanol fuel mixtures use "E" numbers to reveal the percentage of ethanol in the mixture by volume. For example, E85 is 85 percent anhydrous ethanol and 15 percent gasoline.

Gasohol or E10 is a fuel mixture produced from sugarcane waste and comprises 10 percent ethanol and 90 percent gasoline. It is widely available and can be used in the engines of most modern cars and in other light-duty vehicles without the need for any engine modification.

Since 2007, E20 has become the standard blend sold throughout Brazil, and all gasoline vehicles are built to run on this. In fact, most new, light vehicles sold in Brazil can run on any gasoline blend up to pure hydrous ethanol (E100). Pure gasoline (E0) is no longer sold as a vehicle fuel.

E85 is typically the highest ethanol fuel mixture used in cars in the US and several European countries, as this blend is the standard fuel for flexible-fuel vehicles. In the UK and Sweden, E95-fuelled buses are becoming a regular mode of transport in larger cities.

Another alternative, LPG or liquid petroleum gas, is a propane by-product of oil refining and natural gas extraction. Although it is a fossil fuel, it has lower greenhouse gas emissions than petrol and results in fewer poisonous fumes. Most petrol cars can be converted to run either solely on LPG or on a combination of LPG and petrol, which results in approximately the same amount of carbon dioxide per mile as an equivalent diesel car.

Additionally, the natural gas vehicle (NGV) is an alternative fuel vehicle that uses compressed natural gas (CNG) or, less commonly, liquefied natural gas (LNG) as a cleaner alternative to other fuels. The number of NGV cars and buses on the road is growing rapidly, especially in countries such as Argentina, Brazil, Italy, India, China, Thailand and the US. An advantage of NGV is that it is lighter than air, its primary component being methane (CH_4), the lightest hydrocarbon molecule.

Despite its improved emission profile, the use of natural gas faces several limitations, including fuel storage and an undeveloped infrastructure for delivery and distribution at fuelling stations. Natural gas must be stored in large cylinders that can take up a lot of space in the vehicle trunk.

A bicycle being ridden down a street near the Champs-Élysées in Paris. OPPOSITE: *Earthrace*, the world's fastest eco-boat fuelled by 100 percent renewable biodiesel, in Sydney Harbour, Australia.

MOTORCYCLES, MOPEDS AND BICYCLES

Often viewed as a cleaner alternative to the typical car, motorbikes and mopeds with larger engines can in reality emit more carbon dioxide and toxic gases. However, competitively priced electric mopeds are widely available now in a range of designs and colours. Although economical (driving an e-scooter for 50 km [30 miles] is equivalent to leaving a 100-watt light bulb glowing for a few hours) with highly reduced poisonous emissions, the primary drawback is that most current models can manage only up to 50 km per hour (31 miles per hour) and need to be recharged after this distance. New more sophisticated prototypes are expected to be on sale soon.

For meandering country lanes and busy city streets, bicycles consistently come out on top. Emission- and pollution-free, they help alleviate city congestion and keep the cyclist fitter and healthier in the process. In many major European cities, police officers, busy executives and the public can be seen whizzing through the streets. In Copenhagen and Paris, bicycles are free for the taking—and dropping off— every few blocks.

Also, bicycles are becoming lighter, more compact and hence more sustainable too as the ease of transport, storage and use increases. Also, many companies are beginning to encourage their employees to pedal commute by having shower facilities available in the office, further increasing the potential for cleaner skies.

CRUISE SHIPS

The Passenger Shipping Association (PSA), the UK cruise and ferry industries' trade body, says that ships account for 90 percent of world trade and for 1.4

percent of global greenhouse gases. No industry has a greater incentive to ensure the sustainability of the maritime environment than the cruise industry. The oceans and ports that these floating hotels call home are the products they are selling their passengers.

In an effort to clean up the oceans, many of the newer ships taking to the seas do so fitted with the latest energy saving and waste management systems. The cruise companies are working to improve their emissions even further by adjusting itineraries, so that they can operate at more efficient speeds and with more efficient engines. Even the hulls and windows are being coated with a substance that is designed to reduce resistance and improve fuel economy.

The industry has strict rules on recycling and waste management too, and many companies say they are achieving about 60 percent recycling and are endeavouring to cut waste further by minimising packaging and eliminating certain plastics.

PLEASURE CRAFT While the average traveller cannot be expected to understand all the nuances of speedboat pollution, tourism promoters and resorts should be obliged to take more care of their natural surrounds by insisting on the cleanest speedboat engines and prohibiting the use of jet skis entirely. Also, travellers can choose operators that work to prevent pollution, and when deciding to purchase their own craft, they should keep the environmental impact of boats in mind.

The most commonly used engines in speedboats are four-stroke and two-stroke outboard engines. Although traditional two-strokes are more powerful, they are estimated to generate between 70 and 90 percent more

hydrocarbon pollution than four-stroke outboards of equal horsepower. This is because the exhaust and intake ports are open at the same time, and a large portion of the fuel and air entering the cylinder escapes unburned into the water. To exacerbate the problem, this lethal mixture of petrol and oil trails behind the boat, polluting the water and killing marine life.

While the advent of direct-injection (DI) engine technology has made two-stroke models somewhat cleaner, four-stroke outboard engines are preferable in almost every respect. In addition to an improved emission record, they generate less water pollution and are also more fuel efficient (burning 35 to 50 percent less gasoline and up to 50 percent less oil than their two-stroke counterparts). Besides fuel efficiency, they have other benefits as well. Four-strokes are

quieter and easier to start, as they have a quicker throttle response and are simpler to maintain over the long term.

Moreover, inboard-powered stern drives, where the engine is enclosed within the hull of the boat, are more efficient and less polluting than outboard models, as fuel leakage into the water is minimised. Costing fractionally more than outboards, stern drives offer lower maintenance costs and petrol consumption and, if run on biodiesel, are cleaner too.

Although the majority of pleasure boats on the water today are fuel-powered, solar boats are becoming more sophisticated in their design and, along with electric boats, are gaining in popularity for their strong environmental ratings. The ultimate winners for sustainability and, indeed, pure pleasure, are kayaks, sea canoes and sailing.

Picnic on White Rock at
Six Senses Hideaway
Zighy Bay, Oman.
Previous: The award-winning
Earth Spa at Six Senses
Hideaway, Hua Hin,
constructed with natural
materials, performs an array
of luxurious treatments.

ECO EXPERIENCES: SIX SENSES RESORTS & SPAS
To create innovative and enlightening experiences that rejuvenate the guests' love of SLOW LIFE is at the heart of Six Senses' philosophy.

Six Senses is a resort and spa management and development company established in 1995, which runs resorts under the brand names Soneva by Six Senses, Six Senses Hideaway, Six Senses Latitude and Evason, in addition to Six Senses Spas and Six Senses Destination Spas. SLOW LIFE is the guiding philosophy of all Six Senses properties. As a result, the local environment is treated with the utmost respect to ensure its sustainability and that of the local host communities. The health of the global environment is also addressed by the enactment of company-wide iniatitves.

SONEVA BY SIX SENSES—INTELLIGENT LUXURY is committed to offering luxuries of the highest international standards in an environment that nurtures an indigenous feel in design, architecture and service and where nature becomes a part of the guest experience. A Soneva resort has a limited number of accommodations, all offering generous personal space.

SIX SENSES HIDEAWAY is the private pool villa category of the Six Senses brand, in which contemporary architecture merges with the natural environment to give abundant personal space, uncompromised standards of luxury and the finest attention to detail.

SIX SENSES LATITUDE offers a greater number of accommodations than Six Senses Hideaway, while maintaining exacting attention to detail and ample living space. A Six Senses Latitude offers an eco-friendly resort experience with a diverse design personality and a strong sense of community.

EVASON introduces a collection of unique resorts that follow the Six Senses philosophy of uncompromised responsibility to the environment and the host community. Evason resorts are family friendly, while also offering a vast array of guest services and facilities.

SIX SENSES SPAS are a key element of all Six Senses properties and offer a comprehensive range of holistic wellness, rejuvenation and beauty therapies, many focusing on indigenous treatments of their host communities. Six Senses Spas are also hosted by other prestigious hotels and resorts.

SIX SENSES DESTINATION SPAS provide complete immersion into healthy and mindful living and are dedicated to transforming the lifestyle of their guests. Personal life-passages are created for each guest and are supported by a regime of activities and deliciously fresh organic cuisine.

SONEVA FUSHI BY
SIX SENSES, MALDIVES

Set on a 45-hectare (100-acre) island within one of the furthest atolls from the capital of Malé, legendary Soneva Fushi presents an understated yet sophisticated style that allows guests to enjoy the authentic beauty of the destination. Soneva Fushi captures the very essence of a castaway fantasy. Of the 65 villas, more than half offer private pool options, while the Jungle Reserve introduces the Maldives' first tree house. Dining alternatives abound and just about anywhere you choose is complemented by an excellent wine cellar. The resort grows much of its own produce in vegetable and fruit gardens. Moreover, there is an award-winning Six Senses Spa, an astronomical observatory and a PADI dive centre.

SONEVA GILI BY
SIX SENSES, MALDIVES

Soneva Gili is set in a sparkling lagoon, with jetties threading across the shallow waters to 44 over-sized stilted villas and a vast Private Reserve, all featuring rooftop and over-water sundecks. Sumptuous daybeds complement the rustic chic interiors, and all villas feature a host of creature comforts. Several villas feature private Spa Suites. Come ashore for some great dining choices and equally great wines from the Gourmet Cellar. The Six Senses Spa offers everything for perfectly balancing the senses, and the resort has its own fully equipped PADI diving school, plus a variety of water activities.

SONEVA KIRI BY SIX SENSES

Soneva Kiri sits off the southeast coast of the Gulf of Thailand. International guests are met in Bangkok and travel in the resort's own airplane, then take a five-minute powerboat trip. Personal buggies are assigned to every one of the 29 pool villas and the Eco-Villa. A dozen dining options include menus by a three-Michelin star chef and authentic Thai cuisine. There is tree-top dining, a well-stocked wine cellar, ice-cream parlour, chocolate room and bars. A Six Senses Spa balances the senses. Enjoy nature excursions, water activities and an observatory. Cinema Paradiso screens movie classics. The Den is loaded with learning and mind-challenging experiences for youngsters.

SIX SENSES HIDEAWAY NINH VAN BAY, VIETNAM

Six Senses Hideaway Ninh Van Bay is perched on a dramatic bay, just a 20-minute boat trip from the city of Nha Trang. The Six Senses Hideaway comprises 58 pool villas situated on the beachfront, the hillside and over the rock. Several hilltop villas located near the Six Senses Spa have personal Spa Suites. Adjacent to the stunning Restaurant is The Bar and wine-cellar cave. Activities include tennis, watersports and dive facilities, nature trails, gym and Six Senses Spa, featuring signature treatments and indigenous rituals from the region.

SIX SENSES HIDEAWAY SAMUI

Six Senses Hideaway Samui is located on a headland on the northern tip of Samui Island, approximately 6 km (4 miles) from the airport. It features uninterrupted panoramas to the Gulf of Thailand and outlying islands. Of the 66 villas, all with personal butler service, 52 offer private infinity-edged swimming pools. Dining on the Rocks is located at the tip of the headland, with 270-degree views. Dining on the Hill is the all-day alternative. Wines on the Hill presents a large selection from many of the world's most respected regions. The Six Senses Spa offers an extensive menu of holistic therapies as well as de-stress and lifestyle programmes.

SIX SENSES HIDEAWAY YAO NOI, THAILAND

Yao Noi is a picturesque island in Phang Nga Bay that is home to the exquisite Six Senses Hideaway Yao Noi. It can be reached by a combined car and motorboat journey from Phuket International Airport. The Six Senses Hideaway consists of 56 pool villas and pool villa suites, the Hilltop Reserve and the Retreat, which are all set in natural vegetation and tropical landscaping that provides privacy between the elevated villas and still allows glorious views over Phang Nga Bay. There are several restaurants and bars, a wine cellar, a Chef's Table and a Six Senses Spa Village.

SIX SENSES HIDEAWAY ZIGHY BAY, OMAN

Six Senses Hideaway Zighy Bay is set in a secluded fishing village on Oman's northern Musandam Peninsula. It is designed with 82 pool villas, including the Retreats, the Reserve, and a private marina. The resort offers a choice of dining alternatives, from contemporary international cuisine to regional specialties. The Six Senses Spa offers a comprehensive menu of holistic wellness and rejuvenation therapies. Guests have a choice of arrival experiences which include a dramatic drive down from the top of the hill, a 15-minute speedboat ride or a paraglide with the Hideaway's own professional paraglider.

SIX SENSES HIDEAWAY CON DAO

Located in the southeast of Vietnam, Con Son Island—part of the Con Dao archipelago of islands is about 230 km (145 miles) from Ho Chi Minh City. Six Senses Hideaway Con Dao comprises 35 pool villas, plus 16 Private Residences with styles ranging from single-level to duplexes, many with indoor-outdoor bathrooms and several with personal spa suite salas. The Six Senses Hideaway recreates a fishing village and local market, and features truly innovative dining concepts, including the Fishery, Vietnamese Coffee Shop and the Deli. There is a Six Senses Gallery and Six Senses Spa.

SIX SENSES DESTINATION SPA PHUKET-THAILAND

The first wellness retreat conceived by Six Senses draws on 15 years of experience as a global leader to create the premier destination spa of the 21st century. Six Senses Destination Spa Phuket combines the island's natural beauty with holistic and contemporary treatments. The 7th Sense features four unique, interrelated spa concepts, focusing on Chinese, Indian, Indonesian and Thai-inspired therapies, along with fitness regimes. Rates include all meals and two treatments per day. Multi-day immersive programmes enrich personal lifestyles. There are 61 private pool villas and pool villa suites. Wellness-inspired dining experiences complete the journey, with fishetarian and raw food spa cuisine.

SIX SENSES HIDEAWAY HUA HIN, THAILAND

Six Senses Hideaway Hua Hin is located just south of Hua Hin and a three-hour drive from Bangkok. Each of the 55 villas has its own pool in a walled garden, offering the utmost in privacy. The multi-award-winning Six Senses Earth Spa brings a new paradigm to holistic wellness in an authentic natural environment. Restaurant choices include the Living Room, which provides a daily changing table d'haute menu with wine pairings. Other dining options include the Restaurant, Thai cuisine at Kieng Sah, and Mediterranean delights at the Beach.

SIX SENSES LATITUDE LAAMU

Six Senses Latitude Laamu is located on Olhuveli Island in the Laamu Atoll, to the south of the Maldives archipelago. The resort comprises 100 beach pool and over-water villas featuring outdoor rain-showers, water-gardens, private sundecks and relaxation areas. Six Senses Latitude Laamu offers a wide selection of innovative dining experiences, including an over-water duplex wine cellar, where wine tastings and dégustation dinners are hosted, an organic restaurant, an over-water restaurant with cooking hut and the White and Brown Bar complete with DJ, among others. The Six Senses Spa is housed in stilted treatment nests and offers signature wellness treatments and indigenous specialities. There is a fully equipped Dive School and open-air cinema.

SIX SENSES LATITUDE JAFRE

Six Senses Latitude Jafre is located near the charming Spanish village of Jafre, known for its natural sulphur thermal spring. It is just a 35-minute drive from Girona Airport and a 90-minute drive from Barcelona. The resort offers 97 accommodations including studio rooms and suites, many with personal pools and all sharing magnificent views across the Valley of Jafre. There are several innovative dining experiences, including a Spanish tapas restaurant, an Asian restaurant and a fine dining Catalonian restaurant. There is a Kids Den and a Six Senses Spa offering signature therapies that benefit from the healing effects of the thermal waters.

EVASON MA'IN HOT SPRINGS, JORDAN

Like an oasis in mountainous rocky terrain, Evason Ma'In is located 264 m (866 ft) below sea level. It is a short drive to the Dead Sea, one hour from Amman's International Airport and 30 minutes to the mosaic city of Madaba. Its 97 deluxe guestrooms and suites reflect the refreshing and innovative Evason style. Dining options include authentic pan-Arabic cuisine, international fare, a Chef's table, traditional *zarb* in the Olive Garden, plus the Panorama Restaurant, located on a cliff overlooking the Dead Sea. The Six Senses Spa sits directly beneath one of the hot spring waterfalls, with treatments focusing on the therapeutic properties of the mineral-rich waters.

EVASON ANA MANDARA & SIX SENSES SPA—NHA TRANG, VIETNAM

Evason Ana Mandara is Nha Trang's only beachfront resort. Its 74 semi-detached garden villas, many with breathtaking sea views across the bay, combine traditional Vietnamese touches with modern conveniences and are set in private tropical gardens. A diverse choice of dining alternatives includes classic Vietnamese and international cuisine, plus fresh seafood that is cooked to order. The Six Senses Spa focuses on traditional Vietnamese therapies, and the resort also offers tennis, beach volleyball and a water-activity centre, plus a PADI Scuba Diving Centre.

EVASON PHUKET & SIX SENSES SPA, THAILAND

Evason Phuket is set amongst tropical parklands overlooking the Andaman Sea. Just 25 minutes from Phuket Town, it features 260 guestrooms, suites and villas, including 28 with private pools. Four restaurants serve Asian, Western, Thai, and Mediterranean cuisine, using fresh ingredients from the resort's organic gardens. The Six Senses Spa presents a comprehensive menu of treatments for holistic wellness, rejuvenation and beauty. There are three swimming pools, one especially for families adjoining Just Kids!, and a private beach on Bon Island for water-sport activities.

EVASON HUA HIN & SIX SENSES SPA, THAILAND

Evason Hua Hin is located in the quiet area of Pranburi, facing the Gulf of Thailand and just a three-hour drive south of Bangkok. It offers 185 guest accommodations, including 40 private pool villas. All guestrooms offer eco-friendly designs, adhering to Six Senses' renowned responsibility for the environment. Dining options include daily international buffets at the Restaurant, authentic Thai cuisine at Kieng Sah and Mediterranean delights at the Beach. The renowned Six Senses Spa presents a truly relaxing and revitalising experience. Just Kids! has its own swimming pool and keeps children entertained all day.

The Core, the Six Senses Resort & Spa management team, working in the organic garden of Soneva Fushi by Six Senses, Maldives.

ENVIRONMENTAL AWARDS

2008

Spa Magazine Silver Sage Readers' Choice Awards: Favourite Eco/Green Spa—Six Senses Resorts & Spas

Abu Dhabi Urban Planning Council (UPC): First Estidama Sustainability Award—Six Senses Hideaway Zighy Bay, Oman

Wild Asia's Responsible Tourism Award 2008: Winner—the Best of Asia Luxury and Boutique Resort—Six Senses Hideaway Yao Noi, Thailand

Hospitality Awards 2008: Best Initiative in Sustainable Development—Six Senses Resorts & Spas

AsiaSpa Awards: Eco Spas of the Year—Six Senses Resorts & Spas

National Geographic Adventure magazine: The Top 50 Ecolodges—the Most Earth Friendly Retreats in the World's Most Spectacular Wilds—Soneva Fushi by Six Senses, Maldives

The Geotourism Challenge: Finalist of National Geographic and Ashoka's Changemakers Geotourism Challenge 2008—Evason Phuket & Six Senses Spa, Thailand

Virtuoso Best of the Best Hotel Awards: Most Environmentally Friendly—Soneva Fushi by Six Senses, Maldives

Condé Nast Traveller, USA 2008 World Savers Awards: Honorable Mention Preservation Category—Evason Phuket & Six Senses Spa, Thailand

PATA Gold Awards 2008: Corporate Environmental Programme—Six Senses Resorts & Spas

The World Travel & Tourism Council (WTTC): Winner—Global Tourism Business Award, Tourism for Tomorrow Awards 2008—Six Senses Resorts & Spas

Jordanian Association of Engineers, Jordan: The Best Environment Friendly Architectural Project—Six Senses Spa at Ma'In Hot Springs, Jordan

Asean Green Hotel Awards—Asean Green Hotel Award—Evason Ana Mandara & Six Senses Spa, Nha Trang, Vietnam

2007

Wild Asia's Responsible Tourism Award 2007: Finalist—Evason Phuket & Six Senses Spa, Thailand

The Guide Awards: 9th Annual Guide Awards—Excellent Integration with the Environment—Six Senses Hideaway Ninh Van Bay, Vietnam

ATF: Asean Green Hotel Award—Evason Mandara & Six Senses Spa, Nha Trang, Vietnam

AsiaSpa Awards: Eco Spa of the Year—Earth Spa by Six Senses, Evason Hideaway Hua Hin, Thailand

Kuoni Travel: Kuoni Green Planet Awards 2007: Evason Hideaway & Spa at Samui, Thailand and Evason Phuket & Six Senses Spa, Thailand

Virtuoso Best of the Best Hotel Awards: Most Environmentally Friendly—Soneva Fushi & Six Senses Spa, Maldives

PATA Grand Award 2007: Environment Social and Environment Conscience Programme—Six Senses Resorts & Spas, Thailand

PATA Gold Award 2007: Environmental Education Programme—Soneva Nature Trip—Soneva Fushi & Six Senses Spa, Maldives

Board of Environmental Promotion of Tourism Activities (BEPTA): Green Globe Benchmarked—Sila Evason Hideaway & Spa at Samui, Thailand

Tourism for Tomorrow Awards 2007: Finalist—Global Tourism Business Award—Six Senses Resorts & Spas

SONEVA FUSHI BY SIX SENSES, MALDIVES

Kunfunadhoo Island
Baa Atoll
REPUBLIC OF MALDIVES
Tel: +960.660 0304
Fax: +960.660 0374
Email: reservations-fushi@sixsenses.com

SONEVA GILI BY SIX SENSES, MALDIVES

Lankanfushi Island
North Malé Atoll
REPUBLIC OF MALDIVES
Tel: +960.664 0304
Fax: +960.664 0305
Email: reservations-gili@sixsenses.com

SONEVA KIRI BY SIX SENSES, THAILAND

Koh Kood
Trat Province 23000
THAILAND
Tel: +66.39.619 800
Fax: +66.39.619 808
Email: reservations-kiri@sixsenses.com

SIX SENSES HIDEAWAY NINH VAN BAY, VIETNAM

Ninh Van Bay
Ninh Hoa
Khanh Hoa
VIETNAM
Tel: +84.58.3728 222
Fax: +84.58.3728 223
Email: reservations-ninhvan@sixsenses.com

SIX SENSES HIDEAWAY SAMUI

9/10 Moo 5
Baan Plai Laem
Bophut
Koh Samui
Suratthani 8432
THAILAND
Tel: +66.77.245 678
Fax: +66.77.245 671
E-mail: reservations-samui@sixsenses.com

SIX SENSES HIDEAWAY YAO NOI, THAILAND

56 Moo 5 Tambol Koh Yao Noi
Amphur Koh Yao
Phang-Nga 82160
THAILAND
Tel: +66.76.418 500
Fax: +66.76.418 518
Email: reservations-yaonoi@sixsenses.com

SIX SENSES HIDEAWAY ZIGHY BAY, OMAN

Zighy Bay
Musandam Peninsula
SULTANATE OF OMAN
Tel: +968.2.6735 555
Fax: +968.2.6735 556
Email: reservations-zighy@sixsenses.com

SIX SENSES HIDEAWAY CON DAO

c/o 19/F Two Pacific Place Building
142 Sukhumvit Road, Klongtoey
Bangkok 10110
THAILAND
Tel: +66.26.319 777
Fax: +66.26.319 799
Email: reservations-condao@sixsenses.com

SIX SENSES DESTINATION SPA PHUKET-THAILAND

32 Moo 5
Tambol Paklok
Amphur Thalang
Phuket 83110
THAILAND
Tel: +66.76.371 400
Fax: +66.76.371 401
Email: reservations-naka@sixsenses.com

SIX SENSES HIDEAWAY HUA HIN, THAILAND

9/22 Moo 5 Paknampran Beach
Pranburi
Prachuap Khiri Khan 77220
THAILAND
Tel: +66.32.618 200
Fax: +66.32.632 112
Email: reservations-huahin@sixsenses.com

SIX SENSES LATITUDE LAAMU

c/o Six Senses Resorts & Spas
2nd Floor
4/3 Faamudheyri Magu
Malé
Republic of Maldives
Tel: +960.680 0800
Fax: +960.680 0801
E-mail: reservations-laamu@sixsenses.com

SIX SENSES LATITUDE JAFRE

c/o 19/F Two Pacific Place Building
142 Sukhumvit Road
Klongtoey
Bangkok 10110
THAILAND
Tel: +66.26.319 777
Fax: +66.26.319 799
Email: reservations-jafre@sixsenses.com

EVASON MA'IN HOT SPRINGS & SIX SENSES SPA, JORDAN

P.O. Box 801 Madaba
11117 Ma'In
JORDAN
Tel: +962.5.324 5500
Fax: +962.5.324 5550
Email: reservations-main@sixsenses.com

EVASON ANA MANDARA & SIX SENSES SPA—NHA TRANG, VIETNAM

Beachside Tran Phu Boulevard
Nha Trang
Khanh Hoa
VIETNAM
Tel: +84.58.352 2222
Fax: +84.58.352 5828
Email: reservations-nhatrang@sixsenses.com

EVASON PHUKET & SIX SENSES SPA, THAILAND

100 Vised Road
Moo 2 Tambol Rawai
Muang District
Phuket 83100
THAILAND
Tel: +66.76.381 010
Fax: +66.76.381 018
Email: reservations-phuket@sixsenses.com

EVASON HUA HIN & SIX SENSES SPA, THAILAND

9 Moo 3 Paknampran Beach
Pranburi
Prachuap Khiri Khan 77220
THAILAND
Tel: +66.32.632 111
Fax: +66.32.632 112
Email: reservations-huahin@sixsenses.com

BIBLIOGRAPHY

Braungart, Michael & McDonough, William, *Cradle to Cradle: Remaking the Way We Make Things*, North Point Press, 2002

Mas Masumoto, David, *Epitaph for a Peach: Four Seasons on My Family Farm*, Harper San Francisco, 1996

Clark, Duncan, *The Rough Guide to Ethical Living*, Rough Guides, 2006

Gore, Al, *Earth in the Balance: Ecology and the Human Spirit*, Plume, 1993

Gussow, Joan Dye, *The Organic Life*, Chelsea Green Publishing, 2001

Hill, Graham & O' Neill, Meaghan, *Ready Set Green Eight Weeks to Modern Eco-Living*, Villard, 2008

Lovelock, James, *The Revenge of Gaia*, Penguin Books, 2007

Pollan, Michael, *The Omnivore's Dilemma*, Bloomsbury Publishing, 2006

Robinson, Ken, *Out of Our Minds: Learning to be Creative*, Capstone Publishing Limited, 2001

Steiner, Rudolf, *What is Biodynamics?: A Way to Heal and Revitalize the Earth*, SteinerBooks, 2005

Strongman, Cathy, *The Sustainable Home*, Merrell, 2007

ACKNOWLEDGEMENTS

The publisher and author would like to thank the many people who gave their support and shared the benefits of their expertise during the production of this book, including Arnfinn Oines, Remon Alphenaar, Jakob von Uexküll, Steve Galster, Carlo Petrini, Elena Aniere, Tom and Caterina Rossi Cairo, Dr Jem Bendell, Linda Loudermilk, Sir Ken Robinson, John and Cynthia Hardy and Christina Dean. Thanks are also due to all of those who permitted us to include them in photographs for this book and to all of those who gave assistance on location, in particular, the management and hosts of Soneva Gili, Soneva Fushi, Six Senses Hideaway Yao Noi, Six Senses Destination Spa-Phuket, Six Senses Hideaway Hua Hin, Evason Hua Hin and Evason Phuket.

ADDITIONAL PHOTO CREDITS